THE UNIVERSITY OF MICHIGAN
CENTER FOR CHINESE STUDIES

MICHIGAN PAPERS IN CHINESE STUDIES
NO. 27

STATE AND SOCIETY
IN EIGHTEENTH-CENTURY CHINA:
THE CH'ING EMPIRE IN ITS GLORY

by
Albert Feuerwerker

Ann Arbor

Center for Chinese Studies
The University of Michigan

1976

ISBN 0-89264-027-8

Printed in the United States of America

CONTENTS

Preface   vii

I.   The Manchu Conquest   1

   Nurhaci and the Formation of the Manchu State   1
   The Fall of the Ming and the Manchu Conquest   7

II. Ideology as a Unifying Element   11

   Confucian Raison d'État and Confucian General Will. . . 12
   Recorders, Critics, but not Innovators: Sung Learning
   and Han Learning   24
   Imperial Confucianism and the Literary Inquisition . . . 31

III. Emperor and Bureaucracy: The Political Order 35

   Recruitment, Placement, and Discipline of Government
   Personnel   35
       The Roles of the Emperor   35
       Selecting and Motivating the Bureaucracy   38

   Structure and Process in the Ch'ing Government   46
       The Structure of the Ch'ing Government   46
       Manchuria, Mongolia, Turkestan, and Tibet   53
       Military Organization   54
       The Process of Central Government   58
       The Process of Local Government   63

   Politics: Who Gets What, When, How   64

IV. Economy and Society   77

   The Ch'ing Economy   77
       Agriculture   78
       Handicraft Industry   83
       Commerce   86
       Government and the Economy   88

vi

The Structure of Society 94
    Spatial Organization 95
    Family and School 101
    The Social Elite 108

Notes 117

Suggestions for Further Reading 119

PREFACE

Few greater changes have occurred in modern world history than the transformation of the condition of the Chinese empire between the second half of the eighteenth century and the second half of the nineteenth. China in the reign of the Ch'ien-lung emperor (1735-1796) was confident, prosperous, internally at peace, unchallenged at its frontiers. If, to the Confucian mind, not quite the equivalent of that golden age in the mythological past when Sage Kings had ruled, the Ch'ing dynasty was nevertheless accepted as a fair copy of what lesser men in the present age could achieve in the central and perennial task of "governing the world." The Chinese self-image in the eighteenth century--how a literate official or a member of the gentry might have thought of himself and his society--was for that time as close to the historical reality from which it was abstracted as any such idealized constructs are likely to be. True, it glossed over the cracks in the mirror, the fissures in state and society to which we historians are naturally drawn by virtue of our blessed hindsight. But if ever self-confidence was justified by the integration and stability of the society which it reflected, the Ch'ing empire in its glory in the eighteenth century was that time.

In this self-image--which as here stated is, of course, also the historian's construct--China was seen as the geographical and political center of the "world" (t'ien-hsia, "all-under-heaven"); this sinocentrism was reflected in the generic appelation for the country: Chung-kuo, "the Central Kingdom." China's centrality was cultural as well as geo-political, as symbolized in the alternative designation Chung-hua, "the Central Cultural Florescence." Civilization in fact was coterminous with Chinese culture. Those outside its perimeters were "barbarians, but they were not permanently excluded from the blessings of civilization--higher moral values, rules of proper interpersonal conduct, political institutions, literature and the arts--which the Central Kingdom had achieved internally, and willingly conferred upon those barbarians who accepted the virtuous influence (te) of the Son of Heaven (T'ien-tzu, the Chinese emperor) and "came and were transformed" (lai-hua). China's political and cultural centrality, its domestic prosperity and achievements in the arts, and the excellence of its government were seen as consequences of faithful adherence to the fundamental and universal moral principles formulated by the Sage Kings of remote antiquity and guarded and transmitted by successive generations of literate men--who strove to apply them when in office, and when out of office to measure present reality against their immutable standards. The world of China had discovered and implemented the Way (tao), perhaps imperfectly but well enough to discard any search for alternatives.

My intention in this essay is to examine the realities of Chinese state and society in the eighteenth century--before the cataclysmic confrontation with Western civilization which shattered the literati's self-image and sucked China into the maelstrom of a world history in which its t'ien-hsia was no longer the universe and its centrality, up to the present at least, became only a parochial conceit. It would be in error, however, to view this colossal transformation as the outcome only of the "impact of the West." I have stated that the self-image was remarkably insightful, but it was also seriously flawed. In real history, men of learning and character could be denied status and office, and humiliated, exiled, or executed. Officials, high and low, and the local elite might be corrupt and unprincipled exploiters as well as Confucian paragons. The "barbarians" were sometimes "ungrateful" and had to be controlled by military force. Above all, the image was static, as might be expected in a conscious borrowing from an imputed golden age. It thus failed to reflect the accumulating tensions and changes within the real society in which its advocates lived; these as much as the importunate foreigner were to contribute to the great transformation. But the self-image persisted. This persistence is itself an historical fact of the first importance in any effort to comprehend China on the eve of its modern history.

I. THE MANCHU CONQUEST

Ch'ien-lung was the reign title (nien-hao, "year-name," adopted for dating the years of each reign, but now also often used to refer to the ruler himself) of the fourth Manchu emperor to rule China within the Great Wall. His given name (taboo after ascending the throne) was Hung-li, and he was posthumously accorded the temple name or dynastic title Kao-tsung.[1] Ch'ien-lung's great-great-great-grandfather, Nurhaci (1559-1626), was primarily responsible for organizing the Jürched tribes of what is now southern Manchuria into the Manchu political and military forces which entered China as conquerers in 1644 and ruled as the Ch'ing dynasty until 1911. Before attempting to present a cross sectional view of Chinese state and society during the reign of the Ch'ien-lung emperor, I shall review briefly the origins of Manchu rule in China. The larger interpretive issues of the structure and functioning of the Sino-Manchu imperial state which began in 1644 will be taken up in the succeeding sections. Here I am concerned primarily with the question of how it was possible for the populous and wealthy Chinese empire of the Ming dynasty (1368-1644) to be overrun by a relative handful of Manchu tribesmen, and thus also with an example of the general phenomenon of "barbarian" conquest dynasties in Chinese history.

Nurhaci and the Formation of the Manchu State

The two principal factors which explain the Ch'ing conquest are: the invaders were not merely "Manchu tribesmen," and the Ming dynasty had already been decapitated by a successful rebellion when the Manchu armies entered China in 1644 at the nominal behest of Ming officials who sought their assistance against the rebels who had seized the capital, Peking. We must therefore look first at the process whereby the "barbarian" tribes of southern Manchuria were "acculturated" to the agrarian-bureaucratic civilization of the Chinese empire which confronted them inside the Great Wall where it meets the Liaotung Gulf at Shanhaikuan.

The Chien-chou Jürched (as they were known to the Ming) were originally a nomadic forest people, hunters and fishermen, of the same Tungusic linguistic stock from which had come the founders of the Chin dynasty which ruled north China from 1122 until they were

TABLE 1

EMPERORS OF THE CH'ING DYNASTY

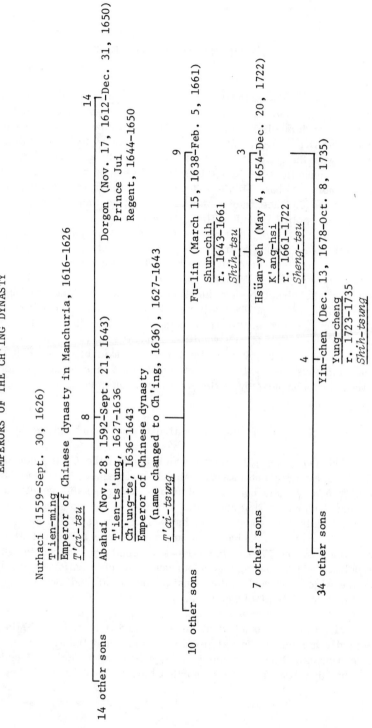

Nurhaci (1559–Sept. 30, 1626)
T'ien-ming
Emperor of Chinese dynasty in Manchuria, 1616–1626
T'ai-tsu

8

14 other sons

Abahai (Nov. 28, 1592–Sept. 21, 1643)
T'ien-ts'ung, 1627–1636
Ch'ung-te, 1636–1643
Emperor of Chinese dynasty
(name changed to Ch'ing, 1636), 1627–1643
T'ai-tsung

Dorgon (Nov. 17, 1612–Dec. 31, 1650)
Prince Jui
Regent, 1644–1650

14

9

10 other sons

Fu-lin (March 15, 1638–Feb. 5, 1661)
Shun-chih
r. 1643–1661
Shih-tsu

3

7 other sons

Hsüan-yeh (May 4, 1654–Dec. 20, 1722)
K'ang-hsi
r. 1661–1722
Sheng-tsu

4

34 other sons

Yin-chen (Dec. 13, 1678–Oct. 8, 1735)
Yung-cheng
r. 1723–1735
Shih-tsung

9 other sons

Hung-li (Sept. 25, 1711–Feb. 7, 1799)
Ch'ien-lung
r. 1735–1796
Kao-tsung
— 15

16 other sons

Yung-yen (Nov. 13, 1760–Sept. 2, 1820)
Chia-ch'ing
r. 1796–1820
Jen-tsung
— 2

4 other sons

Min-ning, Mien-ning (Sept. 16, 1782–Feb. 25, 1850)
Tao-kuang
r. 1820–1850
Hsüan-tsung
— 7

I-huan (1840–1891)
Prince Ch'un
— 7 other sons

I-chu (July 17, 1831–Aug. 22, 1861)
Hsien-feng
r. 1850–1861
Wen-tsung
— 4

Tsai-ch'un (Apr. 27, 1856–Jan. 12, 1875)
T'ung-chih
r. 1861–1874
Mu-tsung
— 2

Tsai-t'ien (Aug. 14, 1871–Nov. 14, 1908)
Kuang-hsü
r. 1875–1908
Te-tsung
— 2

Tsai-feng (1883–1951)
Prince Ch'un
Regent, 1908–1911
— 5

P'u-i (Feb. 7, 1906–Oct. 17, 1967)
Hsuan-t'ung
r. 1908–1912

Note: Plain type = personal name (ming)
       Square type = reign title (nien-hao)
       Italics   = temple name (*miao-hao*)

in turn conquered by the Mongols in 1234. By the fifteenth century intertribal warfare had forced them into southern Manchuria where they settled on the upper course of the Hun river in what is now Liaoning province. In this region, north of Korea and east and northeast of the Liaotung peninsula--Liaotung was an area which long had been thoroughly Chinese in its population, intensive agriculture, and administration--the Chien-chou Jürched were fully exposed to the agrarian civilizations of Korea and China. From the Koreans they learned Sinic-type farming, and after first trading with the Chinese and Koreans for farm implements and draft animals, by the late sixteenth century the Chien-chou (relying on the technical skills of Chinese and Korean captives) were mining their own iron ore and manufacturing not only agricultural tools but improved weapons. Agriculture steadily replaced the forest pursuits as the major element in their economy, and with the new weaponry provided the material basis for the subjugation of other Jürched tribes which Nurhaci, the Chien-chou chief, began in 1583.

Hagiography of the "Great Progenitor" (T'ai-tsu) of the dynasty has by now obscured any possibility of knowing what manner of man Nurhaci really was. Tradition has it that, like Chinggis Khan, he began his way to power in order to avenge the slaying of his father and grandfather by a rival Jürched chief. Nominally the Chien-chou were tributaries of the Ming with the status of a frontier "commandery" (wei) in the Ming military system. That is, the hereditary tribal leaders were invested with Chinese official titles and paraphernalia as part of a Ming effort to protect its northern frontiers against the Mongols and others by co-opting tribal military power into an administrative arrangement which the Chinese could hope to manipulate. Nurhaci succeeded his father as a minor chieftain in this commandery system in 1583. What from the Chinese view was a means of "loosely reining in" (chi-mi) the "barbarians" in order to control them provided for Nurhaci a sanction for consolidating his authority first over the several Chien-chou tribal units and then, by negotiations, alliances cemented by marriage ties, and warfare, over the four major Hai-hsi Jürched tribes to his north. He remained nominally loyal to the Ming, until 1616 avoided conflict with the Chinese and the Mongol tribes, received increasingly higher titles from the Chinese court, in 1590 led more than a hundred tribal chiefs to present tribute in person to Peking and continued sending tribute until 1609, and in 1608 signed a treaty with the Ming generals on the Liaotung border which established the boundary of his domain.

Beneath the surface of tribal warfare and negotiation, and nominal acquiescence to the suzerainty of the Ming, this remarkably able man was also proceeding steadily with the development of the political, military, and economic institutions which would enable him and his immediate successors to mobilize their people for the conquest of the Chinese empire. The Manchu "banner" system was probably Nurhaci's greatest achievement. Although his conquests grew and numerous smaller chieftains declared their allegiance, parochial tribal loyalties remained a potential source of weakness in the evolving Manchu state. Nurhaci's solution to this problem was to retain the lineage organization of Jürched society as the basis for his military organization, but to obliterate larger tribal distinctions. In 1601 the entire population under his control, regardless of tribal origin, was divided into four large military-administrative divisions (gūsa in Manchu; ch'i, "banner" or "flag" in Chinese); each banner was known by its color: yellow, white, blue, and red. Four more banners were added in 1615: yellow, white, and blue, each bordered with red; and red bordered with white. Each banner was composed of a number of companies (niru) ideally of 300 warriors each. The niru in fact were the old hunting and fighting units of the Manchus, their lineage and village organizations, which now were incorporated into a more hierarchical structure. Included in the companies were not just the fighting men, but also their dependents, noncombatant clerks and craftsmen, and bondservants or slaves (largely Chinese captives). While the post of company commander (niru janggin) was almost always a hereditary one, those of banner officers--apart from the top commands which were reserved for Nurhaci's descendants--sometimes were not. In time of peace the bannermen and their dependents were farmers. For garrison duty or military expeditions, a specified number of men were drawn from each of the companies under the command of specially designated officers; the banners and companies did not fight as units. Thus, while it was still characterized by large elements of particularistic ("feudal") relations, the banner system also contained elements of bureaucratic organization which made it a more responsive vehicle for centralized control and direction than the tribal system which it gradually supplanted.

In later years, when the Manchus had openly challenged the Ming and gained or captured non-Manchu adherents, eight Mongol (1634) and eight Chinese (1642) banners were added to make a total of twenty-four banners. Similarities between the banner organization and the Ming commandery system have frequently been pointed to as evidence of the progressive sinicization of the Manchus in the early seventeenth century. It appears more likely that, like the Mongol system of writing which was adapted for the Jürched language between 1599 and 1632, Nurhaci's military-administrative organization was adopted from sixteenth-century Mongolian military practice. Indeed, the degree to which the Manchus had become sinicized and utilized Chinese bureaucratic principles of government before 1644 has probably been exaggerated. A major task of the early Ch'ing emperors in fact was one of firmly imposing the Confucian imperial state (but now with a Manchu emperor) not only upon the conquered Chinese but also upon the reluctant Manchu nobility. Yet, together with the critical adoption of Chinese agriculture and weapons technology to which I have already referred, there were significant preconquest ideological and administrative borrowings from the Ming which eased the dynastic transition considerably. If Nurhaci and his successors were aware, as they must have been, of the history of their distant Chin ancestors and of the Mongol Yüan dynasty (1279-1368), they knew that the Chinese empire could only be governed in a Chinese way.

The opportunity to borrow Chinese political ideology and forms of administration was a product of constant interaction with the Ming Chinese population of Liaotung, and more particularly of the absorption into the evolving Manchu state by capture and voluntary adherence of educated Chinese collaborators who were knowledgeable in the Confucian arts of government. Beginning in 1616 with Nurhaci's assumption of the title of "emperor" (han) of the Chin dynasty of Manchuria, the Jürched nation proceeded with the conquest of the culturally and administratively Chinese territory of Liaotung. In 1618 several Chinese cities and many Chinese captives were taken, among them Fan Wen-ch'eng (1597-1666), a descendant of prominent Ming officials who contributed importantly before and after the conquest to the construction of a civil administration patterned on that of the Ming empire. Before he died in 1626, Nurhaci had established his headquarters in Shen-yang (Mukden), which remained the Manchu capital until 1644.

Nurhaci's son, Abahai (r. 1627-1643), completed the conquest of Liaotung up to the strategic pass at Shanhaikuan, incorporated numerous surrendered Chinese troops and their generals into his army, subdued the Chahar tribes of Inner Mongolia and reorganized them into Mongol banners, dispatched military expeditions to bring tribal northern Manchuria under his control, invaded Korea and made it a vassal state, and personally led the first three of five raiding expeditions into north China beyond the Great Wall in 1629, 1632, 1634, 1636, and 1638. It was Abahai, too, who consciously made use of Chinese forms to further the process of concentrating power in the hands of a single ruler at the expense of the Manchu princes who had been granted hereditary command of the banners by Nurhaci. Three of the eight banners were eventually firmly in his control. In 1629 Abahai ended the practice of ruling jointly with the three senior Manchu nobles, his brothers and cousin; and in 1631 he established in Mukden a civil administration of Six Boards similar to that of the Ming. While the ministers were all Manchu princes, their powers were only nominal; affairs were actually in the hands of competent bureaucrats including experienced Chinese officials. Surrendered Chinese were given high posts, and with their guidance Abahai encouraged literary activity on the Confucian model. A Literary Office was organized in 1629, expanded in 1636, and later evolved into the Grand Secretariat of the Ch'ing dynasty.

On the advice of his Chinese councilors, and in preparation for formally challenging the Ming for the "Mandate of Heaven," Abahai in 1635 forbade the use of the appellations "Jürched" or "Chien-chou" which implied an acknowledgment of Ming suzerainty; his people were thereafter to be known as "Manchu" (Man-chou in Chinese). On May 14, 1636, he adopted the dynastic name "Ch'ing" ("pure") in place of "Chin"--this last being associated in the Chinese mind with the twelfth-century Chin state which had humiliated the Sung dynasty--and formally declared himself emperor on the Chinese model.

The Fall of the Ming and the Manchu Conquest

Thus, even prior to 1644, the Manchus on the northern border of China had developed a military-administrative structure which combined an improved Central Asian-type armed force with at least the skeleton of a Chinese-type governmental structure. As in the case of other "barbarian" contestants for the control of China in the past--the Khitan Liao in the tenth century and the Chin, for example-- this process had taken place in a frontier area between sedentary agricultural China and nomadic pastoral Central Asia or the rudimentary garden agriculture of northern Asia. When the Chinese empire

within the Great Wall was weakened by administrative decadence,
factional strife, and civil war, it was both unable to prevent these
developments beyond its borders and itself presented a target of
opportunity. The semiacculturated "barbarian" states could simultaneously marshal a war machine led by formidable mounted archers,
and offer to the Chinese population a credible alternative Chinese-
style government. Unlike most rebels inside China, and certainly
unlike the rebellion led by Li Tzu-ch'eng which captured Peking in
April 1644 and forced the suicide of the last Ming emperor, the
Manchus were real contenders for the Mandate of Heaven.

The last decades of the Ming saw increasing factional conflict
in which the contending parties frequently were the court eunuchs--
for example, the notorious Wei Chung-hsien (1568-1627) who in the
1620s dominated the witless young emperor, purged his enemies
from official posts, and enriched himself via organized corruption
and extortionate new taxes--and moralistic Confucian officials sometimes organized into cliques or parties--for example, the Tung-lin
party which centered loosely around the Tung-lin Academy at Wusih
in the lower Yangtze valley. From the middle of the reign of the
Wan-li emperor (1572-1620) onward, there indeed seems to have
occurred a general decay in the morale of Ming society, accompanied
or caused by the greed and corruption of the imperial family and
the official class, serious fiscal problems, and an apparent exhaus-
tion of the political system. Add to these classic symptoms of dynastic decline the apparently unusual incidence of natural disasters
in north China--which themselves may have been related to administrative breakdown--and the ingredients for widespread banditry were
all there.

Beginning as a petty bandit in Shensi, his native province, Li
Tzu-ch'eng (1605?-1645) accumulated a large following in Shansi,
Hupei, and Honan from among the peasantry who suffered from onerous taxation, official injustices, and drought and famine. Without
a real base area until 1642 when he established his "capital" in
southern Honan, without any significant gentry assistance, and lack-
ing a social program to consolidate his popular support, Li was
never able to develop a solid political structure to translate his military successes against the decadent Ming armies into a viable alternative to the Ming government. Although he took Peking and in
effect ended the Ming dynasty, he could not hold the capital or establish himself strongly elsewhere in the face of the powerful Manchu and Chinese forces which immediately challenged him.

When the fate of Peking became known, the Manchu regent Dorgon, on the advice of Fan Wen-ch'eng, personally led the Manchu banners through the Great Wall at Shanhaikuan, where his forces were joined by those of the Ming brigade-general in Liaotung, Wu San-kuei (1612-1678), who chose to surrender to the Manchus rather than to the Chinese bandit. The Manchus under Dorgon had already decided to undertake the conquest of China and to replace the fallen Ming dynasty with themselves, the Ch'ing, as the legitimate successors to the Mandate of Heaven. Their forces and those of Wu San-kuei defeated Li Tzu-ch'eng's army as it advanced against them at Shanhaikuan, and then proceeded quickly to recapture Peking. The Ch'ing court was immediately moved from Mukden to Peking. On October 30, 1644, Fu-lin (the ninth son of Abahai, then six years old) was formally proclaimed emperor of China with his uncle Dorgon continuing as regent. The rebel forces in north China rapidly melted away, and Li Tzu-ch'eng himself was killed in 1645.

Not only Wu San-kuei, but also numerous other military commanders rallied to the new dynasty. Shensi, Honan, and Shantung were pacified in 1644. Ming loyalists in Kiangnan, Kiangsi, Hupei, and Chekiang were wiped out in 1645; and Szechwan and Fukien came under Ch'ing control in the following year. A more stable center of Ming resistance led by a grandson of the Wan-li emperor, Prince Kuei, managed to establish itself in south and southwest China in the late 1640s, but it eventually succumbed to the armies of Wu San-kuei and other Chinese leaders who had espoused the Ch'ing cause. Prince Kuei was driven into Burma in 1659, where he was captured by Wu and executed in 1662. The only remaining pro-Ming forces were those which had been led to the island of Taiwan in 1661 by Cheng Ch'eng-kung (1624-1662, "Koxinga") after fifteen years of raiding the southeastern coastal provinces from bases in Amoy and Quemoy in nominal support of the Ming. The Dutch garrison on the island was easily defeated, but Koxinga himself died in 1662. Although this quasi-pirate dominion survived for two decades under the leadership of his son, it was not a significant danger to the consolidation of the Ch'ing regime. In 1683 Ch'ing forces captured Taiwan and incorporated it into their empire as a prefecture of the province of Fukien.

More serious obstacles than Taiwan to the consolidation of the Ch'ing regime were Wu San-kuei and others of the Chinese generals who had played a major part in suppressing the Ming resistance after

1644. In this process Wu and two other commanders had established themselves as semiindependent satraps in south and southwest China. Their armies were large and costly, and in effect they were in control (by appointing their own men to key offices and retaining tax revenues) at least of the provinces of Yunnan, Hunan, Szechwan, Fukien, and Kwangtung. The "Three Feudatories," as they were known, were a serious irritant to the Manchu court, but until the dynasty had eliminated all the Ming remnants, established an effective administration, and reduced the power of the Manchu princes, it could not eliminate them. When the K'ang-hsi emperor moved to abolish the feudatories in 1673, Wu was joined by the other two satraps in a rebellion which again raised the Ming banner and required eight years of fierce conflict before it was finally suppressed in 1681.

The Manchu military conquest of China, if we take Nurhaci's first victories in 1618 as the beginning, thus had taken some six decades. It was accompanied and aided by the adaptation and consolidation both of the ideology of the extinct Ming dynasty and of many Ming institutions, and also by the elaboration of peculiarly Manchu institutions for the government of the Sino-Manchu Chinese empire. In succeeding sections of this essay I treat in turn the ideology and intellectual history, government, economy, and society of the early Ch'ing dynasty. External relations are left for another occasion. I shall emphasize the fully developed situation of the last half of the eighteenth century, but with enough attention to the historical evolution of each of these sectors for the problems and accomplishments of the reigns of the three emperors who preceded Ch'ienlung--Shun-chih (r. 1643-1661), K'ang-hsi (r. 1661-1722), and Yungcheng (r. 1723-1735)--to be evident.

II. IDEOLOGY AS A UNIFYING ELEMENT

How difficult it is to avoid the danger of smuggling the final decay and perversion of an intellectual tradition into its beginnings-- the more so in China where Confucianism and the social practice which derived from it were major targets of the twentieth-century reformers and revolutionaries, and played their final scenes in the comic opera dress of Chiang Kai-shek's "New Life Movement." Even the genuine effort of K'ang Yu-wei and his disciples at the end of the nineteenth century to make Confucius into a reformer was far removed--a century to be precise--from the untroubled acceptance of the Confucian literati's self-image which is described in the preface to this essay. What strikes me most strongly about pre-nineteenth-century China is the universality and depth of commitment to the basic social values of Ch'ing society as expressed in the dominant Confucian ideology. At least among the literate elite there were few dissenters or "Sunday" Confucians. Though he might sometimes be hard-pressed to earn his livelihood, the Confucian was rarely "alienated." These social values--I shall discuss them presently--were firmly based in a philosophical and religious system which itself commanded intense belief. Together, the operational values of the society (which shaped its institutions, i.e., in generic terms its "constitution," "laws," etc.) and their philosophical-religious justification formed a total system which claimed to comprehend the real meaning of life and humanity, a totality that was both pre-rational and far more comprehensive than what modern rationalism can devise. Here was a genuine conservatism committed to continuity not as a reaction to modernist challenges, not out of a sense of previous loss and the vague hope that the symptoms of decay would be removed by the restoration of a homogenous and organic society. Its beliefs and values were not just relative things, but the root of morality itself. Basic beliefs, operational values, and social institutions, in other words, were highly integrated and mutually reinforcing, because through the reign of Ch'ien-lung the system did indeed work--for the political and social elite in any case--to nourish mind and body generously in a society as glorious as that of any previous Chinese imperial age, pace those who hold that Chinese civilization was sterile after the T'ang or, generously, the Sung dynasty.

To the possible objection that I am only dealing with explicit elite values, I must in part agree. The message of China's "popular"

11

religions, which in a sense was the ideology of the peasant masses, overlapped only partially with the "great tradition" which was the creation and salvation of the upper classes. Yet, although gods and rituals may have differed from and sometimes even clashed with imperial Confucianism, even to the extent of inspiring large-scale rebellion in the name of the Buddha Maitreya, the cause was less often that the basic social values of the elite and non-elite were at odds than that the ruling class had failed to live up to its own ideals which it had convinced the ruled to believe were also theirs.

We have in the past also seen such an integrated and unified society in medieval Christian Europe and even into the eighteenth century, although probably not to the degree that it was achieved in China. In Western society this integration succumbed not to any external challenge but to an internally generated secularist attack on the metaphysical and mythological grounds upon which the social values were based. When its philosophical and religious justifications were undermined, the ancien régime itself could not long endure. In the Chinese case the process of change in the nineteenth and twentieth centuries, I believe and shall attempt to show elsewhere, was different. It was not the basic social values which crumbled first before a rationalist onslaught, but rather the political and economic institutions of the society which showed themselves unable to cope with an external challenge. While the social system of China's ancien régime was gradually dismantled, the old values persisted for a longer time and obstructed the reintegration of Chinese society on a new and more just basis. The cultural integument was a tough one; of what was it made?

Confucian Raison d'État and Confucian General Will

My point of departure is the multiform character of Confucianism. At one and the same time, Confucianism was a component of the religious (normative) and philosophical (cognitive) notions which provided the ultimate ground of legitimacy for Chinese social values and the general cognitive framework within which these values "made sense"; Confucianism expressed itself directly in the social values that governed the institutionalization of the social patterns characteristic of Chinese society; and, finally, Confucianism contributed to the ideology which mediated between these values and the empirically observable institutions which they shaped. Thus we may consider

Confucianism simultaneously under the guise of a religion, of social values, and of a political ideology.

By "Confucianism" in this context I of course mean much more that the moral aphorisms of the historical Confucius (551-479 B.C.) as found in the Analects, and even more than the sophisticated ethical and political philosophy of Mencius (ca. 371-289 B.C.). Like Christianity in the West, the body of Confucian belief underwent a complex process of elaboration and augmentation from the time of its founder until it reached its most developed form--in the Neo-Confucianism of Chu Hsi (1130-1200) as in the Summa Theologiae of St. Thomas Aquinas (1225-1274). In this process, the politically powerless moral criticism of Confucius and Mencius became--by absorbing or coalescing with other trends of thought that were once its fierce rivals, in particular the amoral statecraft of the Legalists--the imperial Confucianism of the Han dynasty (206 B.C.- 220 A.D.). And then, again in reaction to centuries of Buddhist challenge and even dominance, the Confucian revival of the late-T'ang (618-907) and the Sung (960-1279) dynasties constructed a rival philosophical synthesis with a heavy metaphysical content in order to give weight, against Buddhism, to the still primary Confucian concern with human nature and the social order. In the early Ming, Chu Hsi's commentaries on the classical Confucian writings were prescribed as the orthodox interpretations for use in the civil service examinations, although Chu Hsi's views hardly went unchallenged by other thinkers. The Ch'ing followed the Ming in this as in many other things. In writing "Confucianism" then, I am referring in shorthand to the whole body of Neo-Confucian thought descended from Confucius and Mencius, as it existed and was written and argued about in the Ch'ing period by both the orthodox Chu Hsi school and rival interpreters.

In the broadest sense, the role of religion in any society is one of supplying the source and definition of the ultimate values which provide the individual personality the means for managing his "existential" tensions, and which give a meaningful coherence to the central social values that define the structure of the society. Religious ideas refer to intrinsically untestable first principles, as do the metaphysical postulates of any philosophical system. For our purposes and as regards their function in legitimizing social values, we do not need to distinguish the two sharply, especially in the case of Ch'ing China where the moral or normative aspect of the official religion and the cognitive orientation of philosophical speculation tended to be merged.

The first principles of Confucianism as religion and philosophy centered on the postulation of the universe as a self-created, infinite, and "harmoniously functioning organism consisting of an orderly hierarchy of interrelated parts and forces, which, though unequal in their status, are all equally essential for the total process." By the time of the Neo-Confucian synthesis, these parts and forces had been ordered in an elaborate metaphysics focusing on the permutations and combinations of li, "rational principle," and ch'i, "psycho-physical substance," some of whose basic conceptions may be stated as follows: The universe is a functioning organism, a process; inherently it is characterized by change. But this mutation is not random, nor is it linear or evolutionary. It is either of the nature of polar oscillations (the alternation of yin and yang) or it follows a cyclical pattern in a closed circuit (the five elements, colors, etc.).

Moreover, the universe is good. "Even what we humans regard as evil--for example, death--is, from a higher point of view, an integral part of the total cosmic process and therefore inseparable from what we choose to call goodness. In short, whatever is in the universe must be good, simply because it is." Man's nature is the essential link between the human and nonhuman worlds, and this nature is equally good for all, human evil arising either from a failure to realize the potentialities of that nature or from inadequate understanding of how the universe operates.[2]

In this philosophical and religious system, human society was closely linked with nature, and nature in turn with the cosmos. All was ordered and hierarchical, and in a profound sense justified. There was no place left open for any transcendental criticism. The religio-philosophical first principles were, so to speak, the templates that shaped the social values which in turn defined the structure of the polity and society by controlling the formation of their basic institutional patterns. "Social values" as used here refers to such phenomena as the preponderance of "loyalty," of performance in relationships of inferior to superior, in the central value system of Tokugawa Japan; or of the onmipresent "success ethic," of achievement for its own sake, in--at least in the recent past--present-day America. The comparable social values in Ch'ing China, which derived their legitimacy ultimately from the above-mentioned religious and philosophical ideas, are summed up, but of course not adequately presented, by such phrases as the primacy of order and stability, of cooperative human harmony, of accepting one's place in the social hierarchy, of social integration. The overriding importance of kinship, of the family, and its deep interpenetration with the political, occupational, and other institutional subsystems in Chinese society may be taken as one evidence of the primacy of these social values.

It is not sufficient to support this assertion by quoting from the Analects or the Mencius, although these classical texts would sustain the position I am taking, since pre-Han Confucian writings cannot provide a full picture of what Confucianism became as a result of later accretions of metaphysical, Legalist, and Buddhist ideas. For Ch'ing China, I suggest that the famous "Sixteen Maxims" of the K'ang-hsi emperor may be a useful source for determining the dominant social values. We may recall that in the first of these injunctions the emperor exhorted the populace to "Pay just regard to filial and fraternal duties, in order to give due importance to the relations of life." An eighteenth-century official paraphrased this instruction as follows:

> Well, what then is filial piety? It is great indeed! In heaven above, in earth below, and among men placed between, there is not one that excludes this doctrine. Well, how is this proved? Because filial piety is the breath of harmony. Observe the heavens and the earth! If they do not harmonize, how could they produce and nourish so great multitudes of creatures? If man does not practice filial piety, he loses [his resemblance to] the harmony of nature--how then can he be accounted man?

The commentator then proceeded to show how filial piety was inextricably related to every other facet of life:

> If in your conduct, you be not correct and regular, this is throwing contempt upon your own bodies, which were handed down to you from your parents: this is not filial piety. When doing business for the government, if you do not exhaust your ideas, and exert your strength, or if in serving the prince, you be unfaithful, this is just the same as treating your parents ill: --this is not

filial piety. In the situation of an officer of government, if you do not act well, but provoke the people to scoff and rail; this is lightly to esteem the substance handed down from your parents: --this is not filial piety. When associating with friends, if, in speech or behavior you be insincere: this casts disgrace on your parents: --this is not filial piety. If you, soldiers, when your army goes out to battle, will not valiantly and sternly strive to advance; but give persons occasion to laugh at your cowardice; this is to degrade the progeny of your parents; --this also is not filial piety.[3]

While the dominant values control the formation of the basic political and social institutions of a society, it need hardly be said that in the actual world people, as individuals and in organized groups, are not merely the passive reflection of these values. They must be convinced to accept them, in the sense of actually shaping their ideas and actions in accord with them. Here is the role of ideology: exegesis, to interpret the meaning of the preferred social values; and exhortation, to invoke a commitment to work toward shaping and maintaining the world in terms of these values. The main body of Confucian political writing, I believe, can best be considered under the heading of ideology, all the way from Mencius' dialogues with King Hui of Liang to K'ang Yu-wei's invocation of Confucius as a reformer.

Exegesis implies both an explanation of the meaning of the social values in question and the construction of explicit social theories justifying specific institutions asserted to embody these values. Such ideological constructs as the five primary relationships (between ruler and subject, father and son, husband and wife, elder brother and younger brother, and friend and friend--all but the last, it should be noted, relations of authority and obedience); the traditional classification of scholar, peasant, craftsman, and merchant in a descending order of value; and the theory of the Mandate of Heaven, provided detailed content to the highly valued social harmony and hierarchical order, and simultaneously justified particular political and social institutions as the means to achieve them.

For the literati, at least for many of them, exegesis also involved an element of exhortation or persuasion. The two were relatively undifferentiated in the traditional examination system and the

course of education in preparation for it. For the mass of the non-
literate, persuasion might be carried on by formal argumentation
and propaganda, for example in so-called village lectures (hsiang-
yüeh). But I would suggest that much more important was the employment of powerful expressive symbols to persuade the lower
classes that the values of the political and social elite and the institutions which embodied them were not merely in the interest of the
privileged, but also represented the interests of society at large;
that the Confucian-trained officials and gentry were the defenders of
common values shared by all strata, and upholders of a natural and
proper social order. Local sacrifices, the local veneration of Confucius and other sages, "ancestor worship," and the quasi-magical,
quasi-divine aura surrounding the local magistrate himself were important means of gaining the assent of the populace to the political
ideology studied and expounded by the literati.

The pervasive effectiveness of ideological indoctrination produced a situation of commitment or at least acquiescence--Ch'ing
society was eclectically tolerant of divergent popular religious beliefs among the masses so long as they did not lead to threatening
political actions--to the existing social order probably not exceeded
in any other contemporary society. Part of the reason for the long
life and capacity of China's political institutions to unite a subconti-
nent--in contrast to India, for example, where Hinduism was rarely
able to provide the basis for a stable political integration--lay in
this unchallenged acceptance of orthodoxy. But the orthodox body of
beliefs itself was a complex amalgam, as I have briefly noted, re-
sulting from centuries of accretions from more or less heterodox
streams of thought. While the basic social values might not be dis-
puted, in practice they were implemented by a combination of detailed prescriptive regulation and discretionary flexibility which allowed over the centuries for creative response to social strains and
gradual change within the main tradition. Confucian orthodoxy, that
is, was rich enough for one phase or aspect of it to be emphasized
when the need arose, without totally negating other aspects or calling
into question the values and institutions of the society as a whole.
I may illustrate this by here characterizing in a preliminary way
the political institutions of the Ch'ing period which will be treated
more fully in the next section.

From the top looking downward to the vast millions of the Chinese peasant population there was the imperial political system. The

traditional political ideology justified the primary bifurcation of society into the ruling literate elite and the various subgroupings of the ruled as the means of realizing social harmony. The classical exposition of this polarity may be found in the Mencius:

> Some labor with their brains and some labor with their brawn. Those who labor with their brains govern others; those who labor with their brawn are governed by others. Those governed by others feed them. Those who govern others are fed by them. This is a universal principle of the world. [IIIa, 3]

Political ideology also justified a centralized administration organized around the person of the Son of Heaven, to whom in theory all proposals for action were directed and from whom all decisions emanated. His role was not only that of ruler; it was also a representative one symbolizing the postulated harmony of the nonhuman and human worlds. So long as the emperor effectively performed the indispensable administrative and ritual functions of his office, and so long as he retained Heaven's Mandate, his absolute power could not in theory be challenged.

The administration of his empire was carried on through a rationalized bureaucratic structure spreading outward from the capital into the provinces and some 1500 hsien or districts. Elaborate rules governed the recruitment and employment of the officials who filled these posts. On paper at least the administrative structure was characterized by a high degree of rationality. Its operations too were subject to detailed prescriptions, covering 1,320 chüan in the last edition of the Ta-Ch'ing hui-tien shih-li [Collected statutes and precedents of the Ch'ing dynasty] alone, leaving aside the multitude of regulations of the several ministries, etc. From the top looking down, then, the political system of Ch'ing China was centralized, bureaucratic, and governed by detailed regulations. From this viewpoint, the employment of political power in the traditional state tended to be universalistic, that is, directed toward the governed as members of empirically defined classes, rather than on the basis of their personal relations with those who governed. Moreover, from the viewpoint of the center, the content of the regulations to be applied tended to be specific and detailed, comprehending all possible cases, rather than diffuse and open to adjustment and manipulation.

Now if this seems to run counter to the common description of Chinese government as being a "government by men rather than government by laws," it is precisely because the complex of political institutions centering on the emperor and his bureaucracy represented only one-half of the Chinese political synthesis. The long-lived and much remarked political stability should be seen as the product of a continuing equilibrium between institutions that can be described as tending in the direction of universalism and specificity and emanating from the political center, and a competing or overlapping set emanating from the local governmental and kinship level that tended in the direction of particularism and diffuseness.

The existence of these two elements is symbolized by the way in which the fiscal pie was divided. The Hui-tien, the regulations of the Board of Revenue, the provincial and local taxation guides, set forth in great detail the fiscal obligations of the populace. It is well known, however, that the sums collected and disbursed in accord with these regulations accounted for only a part, perhaps only 50 percent, of the total tax burden of the empire. This half was the half reported to and subject to the control of the central fiscal organs; the detailed and rationalized prescriptions which governed its collection, forwarding, and disbursal paralleled and interpenetrated with the rationalized bureaucratic structure I have described. But on top of this 50 percent was an additional collection for the most part not provided for in the statute books and taxation guides. This was customary, local, and variable. It was composed of payments of all kinds (whether denominated as tax, surtax, fee, fine, gift, favor, or bribe) largely to local officials which may be subsumed under the heading lou-kuei, "customary exactions." While acknowledged, and often sanctioned by the central authorities so long as the burden was not so heavy as to give rise to protests and disorder, these exactions were the principal source of funds for local administration and for the local officials, their advisers, and petty assistants whose stipends as set forth in the regulations were completely inadequate for the duties they were expected to perform and for the staffs they were required to employ.

The political administration, formal and informal, financed by this lou-kuei, in contrast to the centralized, rationalized and regulated central administration, tended to be local, personal, and customary. In its formal aspect it was represented by the hsien magistrate, a product of the rationalized examination system, of course,

and an appointee of the emperor at the center. But in the performance of his office and in the sources of his effective power he was
intimately tied to local, personal, and customary institutions. Being
by law a stranger to his district, and with his incumbancy likewise
usually limited to three or at most six years, the magistrate was
dependent on local experts and clerks and runners, and on the goodwill of the local gentry for the efficient discharge of his responsibilities. The staff that served under him for the most part was a personal staff, provided for in the statutes but recruited and paid by
the magistrate from his personal allowance and other perquisites.
Finally, the duties which he performed, though broadly defined in
the law code and tax regulations of the empire, contained a very
large element that was either customary or discretionary. There
was a certain looseness and informality about the structure and operation of government at the local level which contrasted sharply with
the center. If government by men and not by laws had any meaning
at all, it was in reference to this second half of the Chinese political
synthesis.

What was true of the local magistrate, who was nevertheless
the formal administrator of his district, was truer still of the local
gentry (and village elders) whose political roles were less formal-
ized than his. The manifold functions of the gentry (shen-shih) carried an unmistakable political tint, although these activities (e.g.,
local arbitration, the organization of charity, grain storage, planning
and execution of public works, teaching in the local schools, upkeep
of temples, etc.) were not formally governmental and were not performed in consideration of any charter of local government issued
by the official authorities. They were, however, the real leaders
(the "ruling class") of local society by virtue of their higher status
as Confucian-educated holders of examination degrees and of their
relative wealth. Although some members of the gentry might attain
office in the imperial bureaucracy, the vast majority were primarily
oriented to their local places and to the maintenance of the "proper"
social order which protected both their elite status and their livelihood.

The "economy" of local political power, from the bottom looking up to the center, was then particular and diffuse. At every
turn, its "expenditure" tended to be governed by the personal ties
between governor and governed--official and subject, gentry and
peasant--while the price asked and finally paid was one that could
be haggled over, depending on the occasion and the circumstances.

The long life of China's traditional political institutions may be seen, in part, as the product of an equilibrium in tension between these two levels of the polity. Whatever the claims of Peking, government of a country of China's size and population from a single center and by means of detailed prescriptive regulations--what one today would call a centralized authoritarian state--was an impossibility before the twentieth century, if for no other reason than because premodern technology, especially in the means of communication, ruled it out of the question. Conversely, a political system founded entirely on the above-mentioned local complex of institutions would simply not provide an adequate basis for subcontinent wide political integration. Both hemispheres were needed; the problem was to see that they fitted properly, a problem that runs through the whole of China's imperial history. Level I and Level II, if I may call them so in the interest of brevity, overlapped in a middle ground where there was room for movement and a change of balance. So long as the change was kept within this overlap, the basic political system was able to maintain a relative stability. Should either level impinge too deeply onto the domain of its cotenant, the stability of the overall political system itself, which depended on the maintenance of an equilibrium between the two, was imperiled. Both the imperial state and local gentry society needed each other.

What is meant by "equilibrium," what kind of "change" is possible within "stability," how could the overall political system be "imperiled"? This brings me back to the question of ideology, from which I departed several pages ago in order to discuss the political institutions justified and propagated by Confucianism as a political ideology. I would suggest that the institutions of Level II were governed by ideological emphases which diverged in some important respects from those that governed Level I. It is not that these two ideological foci stood in stark opposition to one another; it is in fact their overlapping that is the key to understanding the overlapping of Levels I and II discussed above. And above all, social harmony and hierarchical order remained for both the values in whose interest the ideological functions of justification and exhortation were carried on.

By "equilibrium" I mean a condition in which none of the competing or divergent ideologies gives rise to prolonged instability as a result of adopting a completely uncompromising position vis-à-vis the others; in which in general the several ideologies serve adequately to "square" existing institutions with social values; and into which no external pressure has been introduced sufficient to lay the social values themselves open to question.   A drastic change in any of these conditions raises the possibility of a solution that goes beyond the mere change of institutions within a generally stable society. Here a whole society, and above all its political system, is imperiled.

One way of describing the different developments of the same ideological theme at Level I and Level II is to suggest that the first tended to select for emphasis those elements of the Confucian ideology that were primarily political, that corresponded to the interests of the Chinese state as a highly organized bureaucracy, that were concerned with the active ordering of society.   While the term "Legalist" may be misleading, it carries the overtones that I want to convey.   Level II, although it shared much of the ideology of Level I, was more inclusive.   In a sense it can be seen as expressing what might be called the Confucian "general will," which was broader and more diffuse than the interests of the bureaucratic state per se. The Confucian "general will" tended to oppose to the detailed prescriptive regulation of the bureaucratic state the old ideal of rule by moral example, by personal excellence, that perhaps was more in line with the interests of the overwhelmingly large part of the educated elite ("gentry," "literati") who were not actually in office, or not in office at the political center.   The idealization of the role of the chün-tzu (read "gentry," etc.) and of local officials as fu-mu kuan ("father-mother official"), and the preoccupation with one's kinship obligations indicate this emphasis.

In addition, this "general will"--much more than the political ideology of the bureaucratic center--had absorbed elements from the nonrationalized Taoist, Buddhist, and animistic streams which through the centuries flowed parallel with Confucianism.   These tended to reinforce its predisposition to more informal methods of social control.   The "excesses" of Buddhism and Taoism were condemned (as they were in the "Sixteen Maxims"), but their utility as an expressive outlet for the populace was acknowledged.   Even the central government never made any real effort to wipe out these "heretical" beliefs.   At Level II, they sometimes coalesced with institutions that clearly were primarily the product of Confucian ideology.   The not uncommon assimilation in the popular mind of the local official to the local deity is perhaps the best example.

In sum, then, the ideological differences at Levels I and II were correlated with a bureaucratic emphasis on the one hand, and an extra-bureaucratic emphasis on the other--a Confucian raison d'état and a Confucian "general will." The mutual interplay, the tensions, the changing equilibria between these hemispheres-- imperial state and gentry society--and more broadly between the ideological emphases that justified them, constituted a permanent feature of China's political integration.

Within a generally stable society, preserving intact its basic social values, institutional change could occur when one or another of these two trends was in the ascendant. One of the clearest examples of this process is provided by the case of the famous Wang An-shih (1021-1086) of the Sung dynasty. Wang's reforms represented par excellence the interests of the center, of the bureaucracy of what I have called Level I, rather than those of the Level II and the Confucian "general will." That they may incidentally have been beneficial to the "people" is secondary. His opponents, the antireform party, stood in the other camp. Their opposition to Wang was based primarily on the centralizing, overtly bureaucratic character of the measures he proposed. Wang sought actively to reorder society, and ignored moral self-cultivation, they charged; this was not the way China had been governed by the Sage Kings. Again, the fact that the position of the antireformers may be interpreted as socially conservative is an incidental matter. Social harmony and hierarchical order, the highest values, were to be achieved by less bureaucratic, more informal means.

In the nineteenth century, we shall see these same features in the conflict between the "reformers" of several different shades and their opponents. The apparent paradox that it was the leaders of local or regional foci of power, Li Hung-chang or Chang Chih-tung for example, who were most concerned with "self-strengthening" is resolved in part by seeing these regional leaders as proponents of the same bureaucratic raison d'état that motivated Wang An-shih. K'ang Yu-wei, Liang Ch'i-ch'ao and the reformers of 1898 can be seen in a similar light. All hoped to insure social harmony by new departures--including new political institutions--that could be justified as strengthening Level I, but were opposed by those, officials and gentry, to whom Level II was the sine qua non of Confucian rule.

Emphasis on Level II and its "general will" ideology was a common characteristic--I here go way out on my limb--of such apparently diverse persons and groups as Ku Yen-wu, Huang Tsung-hsi and Wang Fu-chih of the early Ch'ing whom I shall discuss presently; the opponents of "self-strengthening" and of the reforms of 1898; and the local resistance to the centralizing reforms of the Manchu government at the end of the dynasty. Such a grouping produces strange bedfellows, but it is a warning against the easy application of such labels as "progressive" and "conservative" when probing the political process in Ch'ing China.

Whether or not all my examples are appropriate--this requires careful study--I believe that it still holds true that the kind of shifting equilibrium I have described was a means whereby some institutional change could occur while maintaining unchanged the basic values of the Chinese political order. If it happened--as it sometimes did as a result of natural disasters, manifest political incompetence and corruption, burdensome fiscal exactions and the like--that neither version of the Confucian ideology could fully protect the existing organization of society from attack, the remarkable integration I have described was threatened. In the late-Ch'ing the uprisings of the White Lotus sect, the Taipings, and the Nien were such occasions. But these were overcome with greater or lesser effort, and in their aftermath the ideology was refurbished and institutions and values "squared" again, if only temporarily.

Recorders, Critics, but not Innovators:
Sung Learning and Han Learning

The late-Ming, early Ch'ing historian of philosophy Sun Ch'i-feng (1584-1675) once wittily caricatured the philosophical disputations of his time: "Chu Hsi's way led to indigestion if one took an overdose, so the remedy was to have a purgative. It was therefore right for Wang Shou-jen [Wang Yang-ming] to advise the people to return to their own minds; but unfortunately the result was over-speculation. The people now are suffering from anemia. What they need is more nourishment."[4] How "nourishing" the intellectual life of the Ch'ing dynasty before the nineteenth century was is the problem to which I now turn. The abstract characterizations of the preceding pages provide a context within which to consider what it was that Confucian intellectuals were actually thinking about.

In any society the intellectual potentially performs one or more of three functions. He is almost always a recorder or transmitter

of the values, theories and empirical knowledge which have been accumulated up to his own time. He may be a critic, of greater or
lesser intensity, of this accepted learning. More rarely he is a
creator or innovator--in abstract speculation, in the arts, in science
or technology, or in management and organization. While there were
certainly excellent recorders and mild critics among Chinese thinkers
in the seventeenth and eighteenth centuries, there were no significant
innovators. No fundamental intellectual departures from the mainstream of the matured Confucian tradition reached fruition before the
disrupting events of the nineteenth century began to change completely
the terms in which intellectual discourse might be pursued.

Many thinkers who lived through the decline of the Ming and
the Manchu conquest were convinced that the egregious metaphysical
squabbling among late-Ming scholars and their neglect both of the
welfare of the polity and of moral self-cultivation had contributed to
the weakening of Ming government and society. Most of the blame
was laid to the later disciples of Wang Yang-ming (1472-1529), the
greatest of the Ming philosophers and Chu Hsi's chief rival. Chu
Hsi's sharp dualism had contrasted "rational principle" (li) and
"psycho-physical substance" (ch'i), and conceived of reality as constituted by one realm within space and time in which li and ch'i
were combined, and a second realm transcending space and time
which contained only li. Human beings possessed a dual nature, consisting of li and ch'i, which through its li linked man with the rest
of the universe. To understand his own inner nature and attain complete enlightenment, the key for man was the "investigation of things,"
i.e., the search for the li of all things in the universe. These metaphysical trappings were intended by Chu Hsi in the main as a means
to enhance moral self-cultivation, a primary end which he shared
with all Confucian thinkers. In contrast to Chu Hsi's approach, Wang
Yang-ming, who also sought to further Confucian self-cultivation,
adopted a metaphysical position which was more nearly a monist one:
there was only one reality consisting of li, wholly confined within
space and time, and it and the human mind were an undifferentiated
unity. Therefore, man could find "intuitive knowledge of the good"
within his own mind: extensive intellectual culture--long hours with
the classical books and in disputation with others, which is what Chu
Hsi actually meant by the "investigation of things"--were unnecessary.
One needed only to immerse himself in action--Wang had a very successful political and military career in addition to his philosophical
accomplishments--and he would know how to act.

Wang's was very close to being a mystical outlook, although he himself did not abandon practical affairs of state. Among his followers the mysticism was amplified and developed into a non-rational and escapist doctrine with much similarity to Zen (Ch'an) Buddhism. It was to this empty speculation, and the useless disputation between adherents of Wang and those of Chu, that the alleged intellectual failure of the Ming was attributed.

Before discussing the leading early-Ch'ing critics of the direction which Ming Neo-Confucian thought had taken, let me note first the majority of early Ch'ing intellectuals who were merely recorders or transmitters of the received orthodoxy. The school of "Sung Learning," as Chu Hsi's followers were called, had the advantage of imperial endorsement. The K'ang-hsi emperor, for example, appointed several commissions for the publication of works expounding the Sung philosophy. Chu Hsi's complete works, with the emperor's preface, were printed in 1714. In spite (or because) of its favored position, this school produced no thinkers of the calibre of its Sung and Ming predecessors, and it had a very small direct (but much indirect) effect on government and politics; few of its acknowledged leaders reached the highest official posts. Such writers as Chang Li-hsiang (1611-1674), Lu Shih-i (1611-1672), Lu Lung-chi (1630-1693), and Chang Po-hsing (1652-1725) were plodding, uncreative men, deeply committed to the moral regeneration of individual members of the ruling class, but in neither substance nor method did they add to the teachings of the Master Chu which they upheld as authoritative. Perhaps one reason for their torpidity was, paradoxically, a weakening of confidence. While they might condemn the mysticism of Wang Yang-ming and argue that regeneration was realized through conscious moral effort rather than sudden enlightenment, the fact is that the reprobate Wang doctrine had subtly come to influence their own ranks as well. The school of Sung Learning in the early and mid-Ch'ing tended also to be intensely introspective, and divorced from practical affairs of government. Thus Chu Hsi orthodoxy was powerful because it was pervasive and not directly challenged, and because as we shall see presently it met the needs of the imperial state. But, by the beginning of the eighteenth century at least, it seems to have exhausted its creative imagination.

The principal critics of the metaphysical orgies of the late-Ming were a remarkable group of men who, in spite of the opportunity to do so, refused to collaborate with the Ch'ing conquerors and to accept positions under the new dynasty. Ku Yen-wu (1613-1682) and Wang Fu-chih (1619-1693) were nominally adherents of the Chu Hsi school, while Huang Tsung-hsi (1610-1695) supported but sought to correct the excesses of Wang Yang-ming. None, however, was primarily a philosopher, and the critical lines of thought which Ku initiated--the effect of the others was small--were significant more for shaping the contours of intellectual activity in the eighteenth century than because they led to new intellectual substance fundamentally at variance with the neo-Confucian tradition. Philosophically, and with respect to both metaphysics and ethics, the "Han Learning" which Ku inspired was largely critical and negative rather than innovative.

After actively participating in the resistance of the Ming loyalists to the Manchu conquest, Ku Yen-wu devoted the latter part of his life to wide travel throughout the empire and to an effort to create a new classical scholarship which would be free of the empty philosophizing of the late-Ming and would produce "[knowledge] of practical use to society" (ching-shih chih yung). There were two aspects to the intellectual program which Ku advanced. First, while he valued moral cultivation, as did any genuine Confucian, he held that the late Ming had given this credible end too much attention, to the neglect of contemporary political and social matters. Nor, secondly, was he opposed to metaphysics per se, but he believed that the contending Ming scholars had been too much influenced by the a priori deductive reasoning of both the Chu and Wang schools. In order to secure sound knowledge of man and society, it was necessary to go back to the Confucian classical writings themselves, and to derive from them inductively the great principles. Ku himself demonstrated the inductive method in his extensive phonetical research into the rhymes of the classics and his comparison of the phonetics of antiquity with those of the T'ang period. His most famous work, printed in its present form in 1695, was the Jih-chih lu [Records of knowledge acquired from day to day], which combined a "positivistic" approach to politics, economics, and ethics as well as to philological matters. The Jih-chih lu consisted of detailed notes which he had accumulated over thirty years of study and travel, inductive investigations of the "facts" from which broader postulates might emerge.

Under Ku's inspiration, Ch'ing classicists rediscovered the commentators of the Han dynasty who, because they were closer to antiquity, presumably had been better able to grasp the meaning of the classical texts, and had done so without the intervention of the metaphysical baggage of the Sung and Ming. The body of scholarship which developed from Ku Yen-wu's initial impetus came therefore to be known as "Han Learning."

Huang Tsung-hsi, Ku's contemporary, also participated in the anti-Manchu resistance movement, and after 1650 devoted himself wholly to scholarly activities. Huang's most important work was in the history of philosophy, attesting to his belief that only through careful critical scholarship could the Chu and Wang schools be adequately evaluated. His Ming-ju hsüeh-an [History of Ming Confucianism] was completed in 1676, and the ambitious Sung Yuan hsüeh-an [Philosophy of the Sung and Yuan dynasties] was left incomplete at his death. Like Ku, he criticized the Ming scholars for basing themselves on the lecture notes of Sung commentators rather than on the classics themselves, and for talking endlessly instead of reading. Apart from this critical work, Huang is best known for his political treatise Ming-i tai-fang lu written in 1662 (a literal translation exceeds my ingenuity; the work has been referred to as "A Plan for the Prince," which gives some idea of its content). This critique of imperial despotism has been taken by some modern Chinese scholars as evidence for the existence of the seeds of an indigenous democratic sentiment in early Ch'ing China. Nothing could be further from the actual case. A Plan for the Prince is a fundamentally "conservative" document, in the sense that it represents the reaction of a proponent of the Confucian "general will," which I have earlier characterized, against the excessive growth of imperial power and bureaucratic rationality in the postclassical age. Huang looked back with nostalgia on an idealized feudal society in the Chou era (1027-221 B.C.), when the power of the center was weak and that of the localities strong, when officials were selected not by bureaucratically administered examinations but by personal recommendation, when the mythical "well-field" system of land allotments allowed both peasant and lord to prosper. If his utopia was inspired by the failings of the Ming dynasty and its collapse, it was inferentially directed against the Ch'ing reality as well, but not from the point of view of a modern democrat. The text is, after all, primarily exhortation; Huang had no idea--there is no suggestion of a parliament or constitution, for example--how he could achieve the decentralization and light government which he advocated and which Ku Yen-wu also endorsed. In the late nineteenth century A Plan for the Prince was revived and popularized by advocates of a constitutional monarchy, but it had no practical influence in its own time.

The writings of the third important early-Ch'ing critic, Wang Fu-chih, were first published some two centuries after his death. Their explicit anti-Manchu racial themes were then exploited by the early twentieth-century revolutionary movement. He was also claimed as a predecessor by the reformers of the same period who were impressed with his assertions that institutions had to be adapted to changing circumstances, and with what they took as his democratic thought (as in the case of Hung Tsung-hsi). In the post-1949 years, Wang Fu-chih has been hailed for his supposed materialist outlook and for his social criticism. But as none of all this--even if it were true--was available outside of the circle of his personal friends during his own time, Wang had no influence on mid-Ch'ing intellectual life.

Intellectual critics there were, then, in the early Ch'ing, but apart from Ku Yen-wu they developed few followers. Chinese intellectuals in the eighteenth century were apparently not greatly troubled, as Wang Fu-chih had been, that the ruling Manchu dynasty was "alien" and of "barbarian" origin. Nor were they usually critical in the manner of Huang Tsung-hsi of the authoritarian political system within which they served and by which they were governed. And I might also note here that they were--unlike some late-Ming scholars who had collaborated with Matteo Ricci and other Jesuits--generally oblivious to the non-Chinese world present among them in the persons of Jesuit missionaries at the capital and in the provinces, and in the growing European trade at the southern port of Canton. Even the two-part program of Ku Yen-wu rather quickly lost its political component, as the Han Learning which he had inspired increasingly immersed itself in empirical philological studies. Ku's inductive method was continued, but in the eighteenth century his ends were lost sight of. True, the flourishing Han Learning was not guilty of the empty metaphysical speculation of the Ming, but neither did it any longer seek "[knowledge] of practical use to society" as Ku Yen-wu had advocated it should. It had become largely scholarship for its own sake--k'ao-cheng, "empirical investigation based on proof"--in the fields of historical and textual criticism, etymology, and phonetics. Philology had replaced philosophy as the vice of the Confucian intellectual.

Some of this work--with which I have no first-hand acquaintance--is said to be comparable to the developments in European philology in the nineteenth century. Among the most important contributors to the k'ao-cheng scholarship which dominated the eighteenth century, attention is usually drawn to Yen Jo-chü (1636-1704) who showed that the "ancient script" (ku-wen) text of the classical Book of History (Shang-shu) was a forgery; to Ch'ien Ta-hsin's (1728-1804) critical notes on the dynastic histories, and his studies of dating of metal and stone inscriptions; to Tuan Yü-ts'ai's (1735-1815) analysis of the ancient Shuo-wen dictionary; and to Ts'ui Shu's (1740-1816) critical study of the Han texts in an effort to penetrate beyond them to the actual documents of antiquity. This was certainly critical scholarship, often directed to proving on textual grounds that the Neo-Confucian cosmology was not ancient, that some of the texts upon which the Sung Learning was based were late or spurious. But it was critical within very narrow confines. It is doubtful that it can be taken, as Hu Shih (1891-1962) and others have claimed it should be, as a prototype of the European "scientific method," that is, as fundamentally innovative. While Han Learning was inductive in its approach, the method of modern science does not rest exclusively on inductive knowledge, but equally demands explicit logic and methodology, i.e., deduction, which was absent from Chinese scholarship.

By the end of the eighteenth century, a mild reaction had begun against the narrow philology and bibliolatry of the Han Learning, perhaps best symbolized by the return of the great Han scholar Tai Chen (1724-1777) to speculative philosophy, and by the development in the first part of the nineteenth century of a "Modern Text" (chin-wen) school of classical interpretation. But Tai's naturalist monism, which had interesting modern overtones in its recognition of the importance of the basic biological drives, attracted no important following; and the full implications of the Modern Text school appeared only at the end of the nineteenth century, when they provided the underpinnings for K'ang Yu-wei's celebration of Confucius as a reformer.

Where is the blame, if any, to be laid if China's intellectuals on the eve of the nineteenth century seemed unable or unwilling to cope with large questions, engaged in no broad social speculation and criticism, were confined either within the empty Sung school or to the circumscribed scholarship of the Han school? To what extent was imperial discouragement or repression of unorthodox thought responsible for the continuation of the "anemia" which Sun Ch'i-feng had diagnosed early in the Ch'ing dynasty?

Imperial Confucianism and the Literary Inquisition

China's modern nationalist historians have tended to attribute the relative barrenness of Ch'ing Confucianism--after promising beginnings--to the despotism of the Manchu rulers. The "Literary Inquisition" of the Ch'ien-lung reign in particular has been made to bear the onus of diverting Confucian scholarship from the discussion of significant ethical and political questions to a passive acceptance of orthodoxy. It is true that, in response to the late-Ming chaos, the Manchus entered China as restorers, reformers, and upholders of the Neo-Confucian orthodoxy. And it is also the case that, because they were "barbarian" claimants to the Mandate of Heaven, the Ch'ing emperors self-consciously felt that they had less leeway than an ethnic Han dynasty would have had in establishing their bona fides as qualified Confucian rulers. To win the assent of the Chinese literati to their dominion, they had to show themselves as super-orthodox protectors of the Neo-Confucian tradition. The Ch'ing dynasty, however, affected intellectual life less through determined and consistent repression than by selective imperial support of those aspects of Chu Hsi orthodoxy--political loyalty, the condemnation of bureaucratic factionalism, the augustness of the Son of Heaven--which reinforced its legitimacy, and by co-opting potential dissidents.

As I have already noted, the Ch'ing like the Ming made the Chu Hsi commentaries on the classics the standard by which the civil service examinations were graded. While some aspiring scholars therefore abandoned this route to status and power, for the great majority the lure of possible high office in fulfillment of the Confucian obligation to "order and harmonize the world" was overpowering. And in the process of learning and repeating the accepted formulae, it would be unusual if most did not emerge as at least mild believers. In 1679, the Ch'ing court summoned 188 scholars to participate in a special examination (known as po-hsüeh hung tz'u), hoping thereby to win the support of some who still maintained their Ming loyalties. Ku Yen-wu and Huang Tsung-hsi, whose names had been put forward as possible candidates, declined to take part. But fifty others were successful and were absorbed into government-sponsored literary activities, the compilation of the official history of the Ming dynasty, for example. Earlier, in 1663, some seventy Chekiang scholars had been executed for undertaking the private compilation of a history of the Ming.

The K'ang-hsi emperor wooed the Confucian intellectuals with extensive programs of imperial patronage for the compilation of literary and philosophical works under the editorship of Chinese scholars. The great K'ang-hsi Dictionary was commissioned in 1710 and completed in 1716. A phrase-dictionary on a grand scale, the P'ei-wen yün-fu, was printed in 1713. Other significant imperial editorial projects produced an edition of the complete works of Chu Hsi (1714), the important encyclopedia Yuan-chien lei-han (1710), the Complete Poems of the T'ang Dynasty which contained 49,000 poems by 2,200 authors, and the 5,020-volume encyclopedia Ku-chin t'u-shu chi-ch'eng [Synthesis of books and illustrations of ancient and modern times] which was begun in 1701 and first printed in 1728.

All this was carrot rather than stick. While the Yung-cheng emperor was inordinately suspicious of his officials and others, and particularly incensed by what he could interpret as anti-Manchu slurs, only a very few instances of actual repression are attributable even to him. The early Ch'ien-lung period was marked also by occasional persecutions against individual authors, for alleged anti-Manchu writings and in one case for taking issue with the Chu Hsi interpretation of The Great Learning (Ta-hsüeh, a classical text). But between 1772 and 1788 the emperor undertook a major "inquisition" which sought to eradicate literature that was seen as betraying pro-Ming sympathies or insulting the dynasty by drawing unflattering attention to its barbarian origins. In all, 2,662 works were totally or partially suppressed, all but a very few by Ming or Ch'ing authors. In the present context, what seems most significant is that, first, anti-Chu Hsi writings were not explicitly sought out for destruction, and in fact--if we take Tai Chen as an example--they continued to be printed throughout Ch'ien-lung's reign. Second, while numerous publications distasteful to the Manchus were collected and destroyed, even greater attention and expense were simultaneously devoted to the buying, borrowing, or copying from private libraries of thousands of rare books and manuscripts, from which 3,462 especially important titles were selected for inclusion in a grandiose canonical corpus of learning, the Ssu-k'u ch'üan shu [Complete library of the four branches of literature]. And among the editors of the Ssu-k'u was again Tai Chen.

The Ssu-k'u project took twelve years (from 1773 to 1785) to complete, included works from the imperial library and newly compiled titles as well as those collected from private bibliophiles, and employed large numbers of scholars. Seven manuscript copies, each containing more than 36,000 volumes, were eventually made and deposited at various places throughout the empire. In addition to the texts which were copied into the Ssu-k'u, the editors wrote critical reviews of the entire 10,230 titles which they had initially surveyed, and issued them as the Imperial Catalogue to the Complete Library. Given the fact that among the editors of this vast project were several prominent scholars of the Han Learning, it should not be surprising that their comments in the Imperial Catalogue sometimes were subtly critical of Chu Hsi and the school of Sung Learning. Numerous other imperially sponsored compilations were undertaken during the Ch'ien-lung reign, among them a fine edition of the twenty-four standard dynastic histories (1739-1746). Co-optation more often than repression, it would seem, was what the Ch'ing employed to win support for Confucian orthodoxy and for their own claim to legitimacy.

It was willing co-optation for the most part. Han Learning was not an alternative to imperial Confucianism; rather its retreat from political and social affairs left the field clear for the court naturally to expect unquestioning allegiance to its definition of the social order from the scholars it subsidized and from officials reared in the orthodox scholarship. The ideal of the scholar-official as a "generalist," as having special competence only in the manipulation of the classical Confucian tradition that guided him in the moral self-cultivation which fulfilled his human nature and prepared him to "order the world" as an imperial official--this was certainly one further root of Ch'ing intellectual conservatism. Like others, the scholar had his proper place in a unified scheme of things. Han Learning, Sung Learning--no one questioned the bases of the status quo. For most of the elite, the status quo--the Ch'ing dynasty under the great emperor Ch'ien-lung--after all worked rather well.

III. EMPEROR AND BUREAUCRACY:
THE POLITICAL ORDER

I have already suggested how the political system of the Ch'ing period embodied the generally accepted values of Chinese society. This was of course a two-way relationship: the values as expressed in Confucian ideology gave legitimacy to the polity, and the state in turn upheld these values and provided means for their perpetuation --the compilation of canonical texts, the patronage of academies (shu-yuan) in which they were taught, and the selection of its officials by examinations which tested the candidates' orthodoxy. There are three other aspects of the political system which I now want to consider: 1) its internal structure--how it recruited, placed, and disciplined its personnel; 2) its formal and informal interaction with the rest of society--how it made its rules, adjudicated them, and applied them, i.e., the familiar legislative, judicial, and executive processes; and more briefly 3) the "politics" of utilizing the capabilities which its structure and operations gave it.

Recruitment, Placement, and Discipline of Government Personnel

The first matter which requires attention is the political system as an empirically recognizable part of the Ch'ing social order, and in particular, the question of how it supplied itself with its principal resource, motivated men to carry out its functions. The search for jen-ts'ai ("men of talent") in the Ch'ing as in earlier dynasties was a central concern of the political process. This aspect of the polity, it should be obvious at this point, is closely related to the question of ideology as a unifying element in Chinese society which I have just examined. To begin with the most important man, the ruler, let us look at the selection, training, and functions of the emperor.

The Roles of the Emperor

The Ch'ing emperors were ethnically Manchus, members of the Aisin Gioro lineage or clan which held a hereditary chieftainship in the Jürched tribes, and agnatic descendents of Nurhaci who had organized the Jürcheds for the conquest of China. One would be hard-pressed to point to any observable physical distinction between a Manchu and a Han Chinese, but in the beginning of the dynasty at least the cultural and linguistic differences were still large. I shall return later to the question of Sino-Manchu relations and the significance of the circumstance that the ruling dynasty of China was ethnically non-Chinese. Here, merely note the fact. Preconquest Manchu practice for the selection of a chieftain had, possibly in response to the exigencies of tribal life, tended to stress proven ability, including military leadership. The designation of a successor to a deceased chief was usually a collegial decision by the leading tribal nobles. In contrast, the traditional Chinese norms (which were often violated) emphasized continuity and legitimacy. Most commonly, the reigning sovereign designated as his successor his eldest son by the empress consort, and the selection of the crown prince was publicly announced as early as possible. The Ch'ing eventually settled on a combination of these two practices.

Abahai, Nurhaci's successor, became the second ruler of the Chin dynasty in Manchuria on the nomination of the senior princes after his father's death. His son, Fu-lin (the Shun-chih emperor), was chosen as a compromise among the several factions of the imperial clan. The K'ang-hsi emperor was chosen by his father when the latter was near death from smallpox. K'ang-hsi--a sign of acculturation to Chinese practice--designated his second son, Yin-jeng, the only one born of an empress who survived to maturity, as heir apparent during the latter's infancy, but in 1712 he found himself reluctantly forced to withdraw that choice as Yin-jeng's mental instability and moral incapacity became apparent. On K'ang-hsi's death the dynasty experienced a severe succession crisis, from which his fourth son, Yin-chen--the Yung-cheng emperor--emerged victorious over his brothers. Yung-cheng, to avoid a repetition of the suspicion which had accompanied his own ascension to the throne, chose his successor secretly and ordered that the choice be revealed only at his death. Of course, educated guesses were made in court circles. Ch'ien-lung followed his father in this practice, and so did the later Ch'ing emperors except briefly late in the Kuang-hsü reign when P'u-i was publicly proclaimed heir apparent. Even the modified form of the Chinese practice of selecting the emperor greatly reduced the role of the princes of the imperial clan in that choice, which was no doubt why K'ang-hsi and his successors preferred it.

At the height of the dynasty the emperor-designate--though he was not formally that--received a rigorous training for the imperial responsibilities that he would one day assume. Ch'ien-lung (then

the prince Hung-li) and his half-brother were comprehensively indoctrinated in formal classroom lessons at the Palace School (shang
shu-fang), were taught court manners and their familial obligations,
practiced certain ritual responsibilities, and were tested with straight-
forward administrative assignments.   The curriculum of the Palace
School emphasized the Confucian classics and the Chu Hsi commentaries; the imperial tutors were scholar-officials adept at expounding
the several main lines of the school of Sung philosophy, particularly
those which stressed loyalty and obedience.   History was earnestly
read, with teacher and pupils underscoring its role as a model or
guide for correct action in the present.   Painting and poetry, the
avocations of every accomplished Confucian scholar, were regularly
pursued.   And, albeit in a largely ritual manner, the princes were
instructed in the martial arts--on horseback with a bow--by means
of which their ancestors had come to rule the empire of China.

Two things might be said about the "vocational training" that
Ch'ien-lung underwent.   First, if the Shun-chih emperor gained a
command of the Chinese language only after he assumed the throne,
his son, his grandson, and especially his great-grandson Ch'ien-
lung were or became--each more than his predecessor--committed
to the Confucian outlook and culturally Chinese.   For Ch'ien-lung,
second, the Confucian political ideal which he took away from his
training was one which emphasized the importance of the ruler's
desire and ability to seek out and employ men of high talent (jen-
ts'ai) in his government.   His image of the emperorship, that is,
stressed people not institutions.   The institutions were given, had
indeed been perfected in the past, but their proper functioning depended upon finding good men.   Ch'ien-lung of course was the autocratic head of a centralized bureaucratic monarchy, and like other
emperors, he could in fact tamper with the political and even social
institutions as much as he wished.   Neither he nor his successors,
however, so wished.   In the middle of the eighteenth century, who
would gainsay that China's institutions were not only unchallenged
in the known Sinic world of East Asia, but as yet also had little to
fear from competition even in the unknown world of Europe?   Ch'ien-
lung was the last ruler of the Chinese empire for whom such a confident assumption still corresponded with some reality.

The roles of the Son of Heaven were multifarious; some of them
I shall discuss presently in more detail.   He was a Manchu ruler
and responsible for maintaining the identity of his people in the vast

sea of China. But he was also the sovereign of the Chinese empire, who reigned and ruled in the Chinese manner. He was the quasi-religious intermediary between Heaven and the social order, whose right conduct and adherence to correct moral and ritual principles assured the harmony of human society with the forces of nature; the imperial sacrifices to Heaven and Earth and the annual first plowing symbolized that relationship. K'ang-hsi and Ch'ien-lung were military leaders who conquered Central Asia and incorporated it into their empire. But the emperor was also the active civilian head of his society: six times (in 1684, 1689, 1703, 1705, and 1707) K'ang-hsi toured his empire, personally inspecting the work of his officials and, possibly, the condition of his people; the Ch'ien-lung emperor, not to be outdone, made six grand tours to the Yangtze valley (1751, 1757, 1762, 1765, 1780, and 1784); and every emperor was confronted with mountains of paperwork and administrative detail. Moral leadership by example was expected from the ruler: the Ch'ien-lung emepror "retired" in 1796 after sixty years on the throne in order, so he said, not to be unfilial by exceeding the sixty years which his grandfather, the K'ang-hsi emperor, had reigned. And we have already seen the emperor as upholder of Confucian orthodoxy and patron of scholarship.

Less obviously, he might be an inquisitorial despot, as some writers have stated was the case in the Yung-cheng reign when the emperor actively opposed bureaucratic factions, maintained an extensive spy network, and sometimes harshly treated his officials. He was certainly always a Legalist manipulator as well as a Confucian paragon: the interests of the dynasty and the state per se brought forth techniques of rule which had nothing to do with Confucian morality--arbitrary judgments, secret channels of information and decision outside of the bureaucratic network, and rewriting the historical record. And the emperor might well become, although not usually deliberately or consciously, the head of a system of "corruption," as when in the last part of the Ch'ien-lung reign the minister Ho-shen (1750-1799), who had the emperor's complete confidence, held as many as twenty offices at one time, placed his own men in key posts, and collected an enormous fortune in bribes and exactions.

Selecting and Motivating the Bureaucracy

While the emperor was a Manchu, his officials were Chinese, Manchus, and a few of them Mongols. The bureaucracy aided the emperor in administering his dominions; in this sense they shared with him the Confucian raison d'état which was the practical ideology of the imperial state. But, given the nature of their training, they were also carriers and interpreters of the broader Confucian tradition, what I have called "general will," which was the property of the whole group of the educated elite from among whom they were selected. As members of the state bureaucracy, the imperial officials were conscious of a common interest with the emperor against the "feudalizing" tendencies of the Manchu nobility, the families of imperial consorts and concubines, and the court eunuchs--that is, the nonbureaucratized components of the dynastic system. And they shared, too, the ruler's interest in imposing order upon and extracting revenue from the "natural" units--village, marketing community, family, and lineage--of Chinese society which lay beneath the thin layer of bureaucratic control which they represented. On the other hand, it is the universal tendency of monarchy to strain toward total power for the monarch, even against his own officials. As a consequence there was tension, too, between emperor and officials in so far as the latter participated in the ethos of political amateurism associated with the "general will" pole of Confucian political ideology. The chün-tzu, the ideal Confucian intellectual, this view held, should participate in government only when the right principles prevailed in the empire, that is, when the ruler did not push too far his raison d'état as against the fundamental moralism of the Confucian outlook. Even while holding office there was a psychological need to adopt a purer and holier admonishing stand in opposition to the necessary Realpolitik of the centralized bureaucratic empire. As experienced from the inside, then, by the active participants in the political system, it was not just an untroubled, routinized, unrestrained authoritarian government. The gap between the ideal and contemporary reality allowed adequate room for what we can properly call elite "politics."

Nor did the state, emperor, and bureaucracy penetrate very deeply into the society which it governed. As I have already noted, "government" below the level of the district (hsien) was largely in the hands or under the influence of the local nonofficial elite, not of imperially appointed officials. There are several different ways of counting, but down to the hsien level about 20,000 central and local civil officials, and 7,000 with military appointments, ruled over a population which in the last decades of the eighteenth century probably numbered 300,000,000. This total, which of course does not include the hundreds of thousands of clerks, runners, bailiffs, jailors, doormen, lictors, "noncommissioned" officers, and the like who conducted much of the mundane business of government in the capital and in the provinces, represents those statutory posts listed in the Ta-Ch'ing hui-tien, the basic bureaucratic regulations of the empire. Civil and military posts were graded into a hierarchy of nine ranks (divided into eighteen subranks): thus the presidency of one of the Six Boards in the capital was graded 1b, the vice-presidency of a Board, 2a; the governorship of a province, 2b; a brigade general, 2a; and a district magistracy, 7b. Officials, too, during the course of their careers advanced through eighteen subranks to which their salaries were keyed. When a 4a post, for example, fell vacant, a 4a official was chosen to fill it. For each rank official costumes and insignia (notably the various colored "buttons" worn on the hats of the officials) were prescribed.

In theory, all adult males, except a few small "outcast" or special-status groups, might attain office on the basis of their personal merit. During the Ming and Ch'ing, most of the legal restrictions which earlier had prohibited, for example, merchants and artisans from taking the government examinations and thus qualifying for office, were removed. In the eighteenth century, "merit" still meant primarily success in the civil service examinations. Officials of the third rank and above had the privilege of nominating their sons for government service without examination, but this yin ("recommendation") system was only of very minor importance in the Ch'ing as compared to earlier periods. Official titles, in particular that of chien-sheng (student in the Imperial Academy), and sometimes actual offices were sold in the Ch'ing on a much grander scale than in the Ming. Even in the eighteenth century, money might thus sometimes provide a direct route of entry into at least local office, but the really significant sale of titles and offices occurred only after the middle of the nineteenth century in response to the dynasty's need for funds to meet the threat of the Taiping and other rebellions.

Indirectly, however, the wealth of one's family or lineage was an important determinant of who could compete successfully in the government examinations. Mastery of the Chinese written language (literary style and calligraphy) and of the Confucian classics and their commentaries--these were what was principally tested--required substantial leisure for study and could be aided by a strict tutor.

Needless to say, sons of wealthier families had greater leisure, and in the normal course of things, a well-to-do lineage would have established a local private school for the aspiring scholars among its kinsmen. The really bright son of a poor peasant family, if his lineage or village (the two often coincided) had provided tutors in this way, might also "make it," but not very often.

Especially in the Ming period (overall average 47.5 percent), but also to a lesser extent in the Ch'ing (19.1 percent), the evidence indicates that a substantial proportion of those who obtained the coveted chin-shih degree came from families which for three preceding generations had produced no chien-sheng or sheng-yuan and no office holders. There was thus surely considerable upward--and downward--mobility into and out of the lower strata of the gentry, but this process typically was mediated by the accumulation and dispersion of landed wealth accompanied by a parallel growth or decline of a scholarly commitment within the family. The absence of primogeniture, the practice of fen-chia (division of family holdings roughly equally among all the male heirs), the economic precariousness of small-scale agriculture, and the more or less random distribution of academic talent in the populace: these factors contributed to considerable status mobility for individual families while the whole class of the local elite maintained its size, its disproportionate share of total wealth, and its dominance of local society.

The lowest academic degree, sheng-yuan, was awarded for success in the local examinations. It was an honorable thing, exempted its holder from the corvee tax obligation, and gave his family status in their locality, i.e., made them part of the local "gentry." But it brought no official appointment. Neither did the chien-sheng title, although it too conferred an exemption from the labor service tax and gentry status in one's home locality. Some sheng-yuan, a small fraction, on the basis of either seniority or merit might be awarded the kung-sheng degree, and possibly an eventual minor appointment. Successful candidates in the triennial provincial examinations won the chü-jen degree, high status, and like the kung-sheng, possibly a minor office in the future. But most important, the chü-jen won the opportunity to compete in the triennial examinations held in the capital for the highest degree, the chin-shih. Success in this metropolitan examination, and in the palace examination which immediately followed, almost automatically guaranteed an appointment in the middle ranks of the imperial bureaucracy.

How many made it? In the first part of the nineteenth century, the average number of chin-shih degrees awarded at each examination was 211, while the chü-jen average was about 1,400. For the local sheng-yuan examinations, which were held twice in each three-year period, the quota of degrees to be awarded was 25,000 at each occasion. If we take a typical year in the 1830s, when the Chinese population probably totalled 400,000,000, the number of living holders of civil degrees, listed by the highest degree held, might have been approximately as follows: chin-shih, 2,500; chü-jen, 18,000; kung-sheng, 27,000; chien-sheng, 310,000; and sheng-yuan, 460,000. There were in addition perhaps 210,000 holders of military degrees, of which about 15,000 were higher degrees which could qualify for office.

Thus out of something over a million degree holders alive at one time, only 47,500 had higher civil degrees and 15,000 higher military degrees which made them eligible for official appointments. Of these men, a little less than half were actually in office, if we use the 27,000 figure for office holders suggested above. The rest were either retired officials, expectant officials, advisers to provincial and local office holders (mu-yu, "tent-friends"), or disappointed nonofficials.

The Manchu conquest meant, among other things, that the number of positions at the top of the bureaucratic hierarchy open to meritorious Han Chinese was somewhat reduced. In the important offices in the capital, roughly an equal number of Chinese and non-Chinese (Manchus and Mongols) were employed throughout the Ch'ing period. While earlier in the dynasty few Manchus qualified for high office via the government examinations, by the mid-eighteenth century a fair number of the non-Chinese in the metropolitan bureaucracy held chü-jen or chin-shih degrees. Local government posts in China proper were almost exclusively held by Chinese appointees, while in Central Asia and other non-Chinese parts of the empire, Manchus, Mongols, and local ethnic representatives were overwhelmingly dominant. The ethnic composition of the holders of the key provincial positions of governor-general and governor, however, underwent several shifts in the course of the dynasty, which are shown in Table 2.

For the whole of the period 1644-1911, Han Chinese and Chinese bannermen (those Chinese who had early gone over to the Manchu

cause and were enrolled in banner units) constituted 70.6 percent of
the total number of governors-general and governors, Manchu appointees, 27.3 percent, and Mongols, a negligible 2.1 percent. In the
seventeenth century, however, before the Manchu conquest was
consolidated, Chinese bannermen dominated these positions. The
implication is that early in the dynasty, before many Manchus had
developed the literary and bureaucratic qualifications to govern in
a Chinese manner, the Ch'ing relied heavily upon those Chinese who
had demonstrated their loyalty (and were looked upon scornfully as
"collaborators" by many other Chinese) to the throne. In the eighteenth century, the percentage of Manchus increased sharply and so
to a lesser extent did the proportion of Han Chinese--both at the
expense of the Chinese bannermen--until they were nearly equal in
the years 1736-1795. Obviously the Manchu elite had become more
"sinicized," while the ethnic Chinese as a whole had come to accept
the dynasty. The proportion of Han Chinese continued to increase
in the nineteenth century, but the Manchu component dropped from
48 percent in the period 1736-1795 to 29.6 percent in the first half
of the nineteenth century and then to 19.7 percent in the second half.
Even if these data are qualified by noting that Manchu governors-
general had average tenures in a single post of 33 months and average total service of 58 months, while Han Chinese appointees served
on the average 32 months and saw average total service of 54 months
(the comparable figures for governors are: Manchus, 25 months and
47 months; Chinese, 26 months and 44 months), the picture of initial
dominance by Chinese bannermen, then a slight edge for Manchus,
and lastly a growing Chinese role, in the seventeenth, eighteenth,
and nineteenth centuries respectively, is not greatly altered.

Why this sequence? I have already suggested that the eighteenth century was one of great dynastic self-confidence, when the
Ch'ing social order functioned well internally and external threats
were competently removed. Manchu officials trained in Chinese
bureaucratic ways became more numerous, and they could be trusted
with the routine maintenance of a successfully operating polity. This
configuration changed in the nineteenth century, a period marked by
intense military and economic pressure from the West and by the
outbreak of serious domestic rebellion. In this new situation, the
dynasty became reluctantly aware that the responsibilities which had
been assigned to Manchu provincial officials exceeded the talents
that were available. Even more than their Chinese counterparts,
Manchu officials, because they were Manchu and self-consciously

TABLE 2

ETHNIC ORIGINS OF GOVERNORS-GENERAL AND GOVERNORS

		Total New Personnel		Han Chinese		Chinese Bannermen		Manchus		Mongols	
		Number	%	Number	%	Number	%	Number	%	Number	%
1644–1683	Governors-General	79	100.0	13	16.4	56	70.9	10	12.7	–	–
	Governors	190	100.0	45	23.7	131	68.9	14	7.4	–	–
	Total	269	100.0	58	21.6	187	69.5	24	8.9	–	–
1684–1735	Governors-General	103	100.0	30	29.1	39	37.9	34	33.0	–	–
	Governors	245	100.0	91	37.2	88	35.9	64	26.1	2	0.8
	Total	348	100.0	121	34.8	127	36.5	98	28.2	2	0.5
1736–1795	Governors-General	109	100.0	34	31.2	8	7.3	63	57.8	4	3.7
	Governors	222	100.0	107	48.2	16	7.2	96	43.2	3	1.4
	Total	331	100.0	141	42.6	24	7.3	159	48.0	7	2.1
1796–1850	Governors-General	133	100.0	76	57.1	7	5.3	45	33.8	5	3.8
	Governors	199	100.0	129	64.8	9	4.5	53	26.7	8	4.0
	Total	332	100.0	205	61.7	16	4.8	98	29.6	13	3.9
1851–1911	Governors-General	130	100.0	85	65.4	5	3.8	35	27.0	5	3.8
	Governors	266	100.0	207	77.8	8	3.0	43	16.2	8	3.0
	Total	396	100.0	292	73.7	13	3.3	78	19.7	13	3.3
1644–1911 (Ch'ing as a whole)	Governors-General	554	100.0	238	43.0	115	20.8	187	33.7	14	2.5
	Governors	1122	100.0	579	51.6	252	22.4	270	24.1	21	1.9
	Total	1676	100.0	817	48.7	367	21.9	457	27.3	35	2.1

Source: Adapted from Tables 5 and 6 in Lawrence D. Kessler, "Ethnic Composition of Provincial Leadership during the Ch'ing Period," The Journal of Asian Studies, 28.3 (May 1969), pp. 489–511.

that, tended to be conservative and plodding and safely orthodox in circumstances which now required boldness and adaptability. Hence the court moved to increase the Chinese component at the top of the strategic provincial bureaucracies. Survival for the ruler and the dynasty was a more important end than survival of what was already a very much diluted Manchu culture.

Once qualified by examination (or purchase), the candidate for office was required to seek an imperial audience before his claim to employment would be recognized by the Board of Civil Appointments or the Board of War, for civil and military posts respectively. Nominally every official down to the hsien magistrate was appointed by the emperor, but in practice the lower posts were assigned by the two Boards. In many cases the initial appointment for local and sub-provincial posts up to that of taotai (circuit intendent) was as an "expectant" official only, pending a substantive opening. By a strict rule of avoidance, officials could not hold office in the provinces of their birth, nor were closely related persons permitted to serve in the same bureau or province. Detailed service records were maintained by the Board of Civil Appointments; at the end of his normal three-year tenure in office an official's personal conduct and administrative performance were examined--strictly in the case of those below the fifth rank, usually only perfunctorily for the higher bureaucrats, many of whom were personally known to the emperor. These examinations could result in promotion, reappointment, demotion, or dismissal.

Discipline and bureaucratic effectiveness were achieved by a combination of external control and the bureaucrat's internalized self-image. The techniques of control included imperial support of ideological orthodoxy, regular evaluations of official performance as I have just indicated, the ever-present possibility of indictment by the censorate, a strict administrative code--which although exacting in its demands prescribed relatively mild specific penalties, and the frequent utilization of the devices of plural offices for one man, several men for one office (e.g., two presidents and four vice-presidents of the Six Boards), and several offices for one function (e.g., governors-general and governors)--checks and balances to prevent the concentration of bureaucratic power. The bureaucrat's self-image was a product of the classical education he had received and of his commitment to Confucian political values. As I suggested earlier, there was sufficient ambiguity in those values for the traditional and limited task of government to be handled with some flexibility. A Confucian serving the Legalist-Confucian state could never be fully satisfied that the mundane present actualized the morality of the Sage Kings. Hence there was room for complex argument about which were the best policies and organizational forms, and space too for some change within the tradition. Fundamental political change in response to problems and conditions which the classical learning had not envisaged was, however, beyond the capacity of the system.

Structure and Process in the Ch'ing Government

Did the Ch'ing empire have a "constitution"? In the sense of a document drawn up by a representative deliberative body and ratified by the political constituency, the answer of course is no. If, however, we think in functional rather than formal terms, and define constitution as a body of generally accepted norms which demarcate the goals, organizational structure, and operating procedures of the political system, then indeed there was a Ch'ing constitution. In order of increasing specificity, these norms were expressed in the orthodox Confucian political ideology, imperial decisions which became precedents difficult to violate, and the formally compiled and printed Ta-Ch'ing Hui-tien (Collected statutes of the Ch'ing dynasty. Five editions: 1690, 162 chüan or "books"; 1733, 250 chüan; 1767, 100 chüan plus 180 chüan of tse-li ["regulations"]; 1818, 80 chüan plus 920 chüan of shih-li ["precedents"] and 132 chüan of illustrations; 1899, 100 chüan plus 1,220 chüan of shih-li and 270 chüan of illustrations). This constitution did not provide for popular political participation, define civil rights, or protect the liberty and property of the subjects of the empire from arbitrary violation by the ruler. These of course were a range of considerations outside of the scope of the political process in pre-twentieth-century China. Ideology, imperial precedents, and the published fundamental statutes did, however, establish a particular type of government whose structure and procedures were clearly articulated and not subject to willful or capricious alteration.

The Structure of the Ch'ing Government

Broadly speaking, the legislative and executive functions of the Ch'ing state were indistinguishable. In the course of the administrative process itself, the emperor made executive decisions which became the basic laws of the realm. Within this context other executives--governors-general or the administrators of the galt gabelle, for example--also made decisions which had the force of laws of more limited scope. In the first part of the dynasty, the imperial rule-making function was subject to the hereditary power of the Manchu princes based in part on their personal command of five of the eight banners. When in 1667 the young K'ang-hsi emperor took over control of his government from the regents who had ruled during his minority, he made some progress in reducing the influence of the Manchu nobles. K'ang-hsi's enhancement of Chinese-style imperial-bureaucratic forms of rule is symbolized by the publication of the first edition of the Hui-tien in 1690. However, the Council of Deliberative Princes and Ministers, which continued the practice of consultation with the nobles which went back to the time of Nurhaci, retained substantial powers, and the banners were not yet fully under imperial command. The Yung-cheng emperor, in view of his own contest with princely rivals to succeed his father, proceeded with determination and success to curtail any independent role for the nobility. In addition to placing the banners under his control, Yung-cheng's principal device to this end was the development between 1729 and 1731 of the Grand Council (Chün-chi-ch'u) into the primary advisory, secretarial, and coordinating body for the emperor. In this respect it also took over most of the powers of the Grand Secretariat (Nei-ko), an institution inherited from the Ming, which was left with only routine functions but much honor. The Grand Council came into being as the emperor's supreme headquarters for the military campaigns then being directed against the Mongols, the kind of issue which earlier had called for extended consultations with the Manchu nobility. In contrast, the new Grand Council was made up entirely of high bureaucrats holding other metropolitan offices concurrently; their number was unspecified, but it was very often five or six. Sixty secretaries, half Chinese and half Manchus, handled its clerical tasks. Of the 145 Councillors appointed between 1730 and 1911, 72 were Manchus including nine princes, 64 Chinese, three Chinese bannermen, and six Mongols.

Much of the staff work for the emperor, on the basis of which he was able to act on the matters which the Grand Council laid before him, was performed by the Six Boards or Ministries (Liu-pu). In the Ming period, the Boards had had greater executive functions. But in the Ch'ing, they were staff rather than line

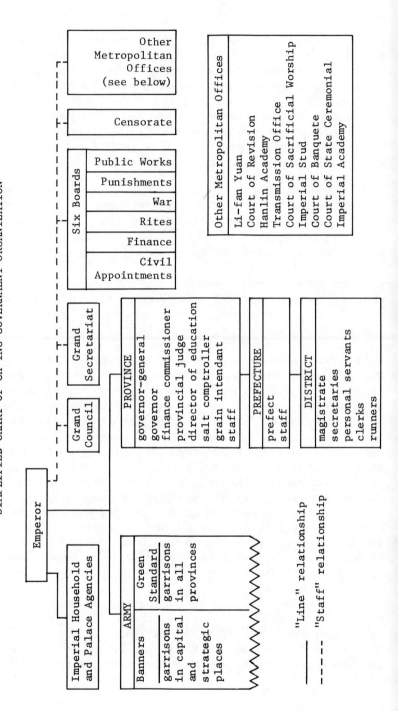

TABLE 3

SIMPLIFIED CHART OF CH'ING GOVERNMENT ORGANIZATION

offices with little direct influence on provincial government, which
next to the emperor himself was the chief locus of decision-making.
In the order of their status, the Six Boards were: Civil Appointments (Li-pu), whose functions I have already described; Revenue
(Hu-pu), which directed the collection of taxes and their disburse-
ment, maintained the coinage, and supervised the customs houses,
granaries, and treasuries; Rites or Ceremonies (Li-pu), supervision
of state ceremonies, tribute-bearing emissaries, various ritual
matters, and the civil service examinations; War (Ping-pu), in
charge of military examinations, the appointment, promotion, and
dismissal of military officials, and the postal relay system; Punishments (Hsing-pu), supervision and review of criminal cases; and
Public Works (Kung-pu), which oversaw the construction and maintenance of buildings, bridges, canals, etc., and the manufacture of
arms, silk textiles for the court, and the like. The Six Boards,
with their accumulated precedents and their removal from direct
administration--the Board of War commanded no troops and the
Board of Revenue did not collect the revenue through its own agents
--tended to be a locus of conservatism in the central government,
increasingly so in the nineteenth century. Each was headed by two
presidents, one Chinese and one Manchu, and by two Chinese and
two Manchu vice-presidents--an excess of collegiality which could
lead to an equal quantity of indecisiveness.

Also part of the central administration was the Censorate (Tu-
ch'a yuan), charged with the dual responsibilities of remonstrating
with the emperor and investigating and impeaching malefactions in
the central and provincial bureaucracies. Its personnel consisted
of an equal number of Chinese and Manchus. Twenty-four censors
were attached to the Six Boards, ten others to various precincts of
the city of Peking, and 56 to the provinces where they were distributed in fifteen circuits. While in earlier eras there had indeed
been a tradition of censors speaking out frankly even in criticism
of the emperor, this function atrophied into insignificance in the
Ch'ing. The ferreting out of official incompetence or corruption
was sometimes done well, but in the latter part of the dynasty the
Censorate like the Six Boards was identified with a strongly conservative outlook.

With the exception of the Grand Council and the duplication of
the top posts in order to accommodate a Manchu component equal
to the Chinese, the organization of the central government had been

copied by the Ch'ing from its Ming predecessor. Numerous additional minor offices, again mainly modelled on Ming practice, were also located in Peking, but they need not detain us here. In the middle of the nineteenth century, a few significant additions were made to the metropolitan administration--notably the Tsungli Yamen and the Imperial Maritime Customs; toward the end of the dynasty a wholesale reorganization was begun. (I shall discuss these in another essay.)

The Ch'ing provincial administration consisted of three main parts, each with its separate style of government: the provinces of China proper; Manchuria--the dynastic homeland; and Tibet, Mongolia, and Turkestan. China within the Great Wall was divided into eighteen provinces, each of which except Chihli and Szechwan had its governor (hsün-fu). The administration of the metropolitan province of Chihli and of Szechwan in the west, because of their strategic importance, was in each case headed by a governor-general (tsung-tu). With the exception of the three provinces of Shantung, Honan, and Shansi, governors-general were appointed to administer--in association with their governors--groups of two, or in one case three, of the remaining provinces: Liang-Chiang governor-general, Kiangsu, Anhwei, and Kiangsi; Shen-Kan governor-general, Shensi and Kansu; Min-Che governor-general, Fukien and Chekiang; Hu-Kuang governor-general, Hupei and Hunan; Liang-Kuang governor-general, Kwangtung and Kwangsi; and Yun-Kuei governor-general, Yunnan and Kweichow. This arrangement reached its final form in 1748 after some experimentation in the first part of the dynasty.

The Ch'ing governors and governors-general had evolved directly from the late-Ming delegation of officials from the capital to coordinate the administrative offices and surveillance offices which comprised the key parts of provincial government in the Ming. Ch'ing provincial financial commissioners or treasurers (pu-cheng-shih), and provincial judges (an-ch'a-shih), bore the same names as their Ming predecessors, the heads of the administration and surveillance offices, but were now subordinated to the governors-general and governors and performed staff rather than line duties. They continued to receive their appointments directly from the emperor and to have the nominal right to memorialize the throne, but this right was much circumscribed in practice by the mid-eighteenth century and became even more so in the mid-nineteenth. Other high provincial officials were the educational directors, and the salt comptrollers and grain intendants, in charge respectively of the salt monopoly and tribute grain shipments--their incidence and responsibilities varied from province to province. While the governor, ranked 2b, was technically subordinate to the governor-general, ranked 2a, the two in practice were usually co-equal and sometimes in conflict. Their joint presence in all of the provinces but five was part of a system of elaborate checks and balances which the Manchu conquerors had instituted as a means of preventing any concentration of power which might subvert the authority of the emperor and dynasty.

Although the actual table of organization was somewhat more complex--for example, I have omitted discussion of the 84 circuits in China proper, each comprising a part of a province usually larger than a prefecture and each headed by a circuit intendant (tao-t'ai) --it is not a great distortion to state that there were two levels of formal government beneath the provinces. Each province was divided into prefectures (fu), about 180 in total; and the fu in turn were divided into about 1,500 departments (chou) and districts or counties (hsien), the latter being by far the more numerous. The prefects and the department or district magistrates were invested with office by the emperor, and assigned to the various provinces by the Board of Civil Appointments, but actually appointed to substantive office on the recommendation of the governors-general and governors. They carried out their responsibilities under the direct supervision and control of the higher provincial authorities.

The district, in some cases subdistricts, was as far as the formal structure of imperial government extended. Its magistrate was placed at the interface between the imperial state and the largely rural society which it governed. As the emperor's appointee he was the nearly absolute ruler of a district whose population might be 250,000 or more. His responsibilities--for collecting the tax quotas, for maintaining order, for all that happened in his jurisdiction-- were as great as his nominal authority. To the degree that he was successful, he was dependent upon the cooperation of the social elite of his locality, a matter to which I shall return presently. At various times, but with indifferent success, the imperial state attempted to extend its influence directly into the local society, to bypass or at least limit the domination of the rural gentry. Its principal devices to this end were the pao-chia (rural surveillance) and li-chia (revenue collection) systems.

With adaptations and refinements, the Ch'ing took over the Ming pao-chia and li-chia. In effect these were efforts to super-impose imperially defined "artificial" administrative subdivisions upon the "natural" divisions of rural society. Nomenclature and practice were complex and changing, so that the following remarks are to be understood as a considerable simplification. The Ch'ing pao-chia was designed to count the number and watch the activities and movements of the rural population by means of nonelite agents selected by the populace itself and confirmed by the magistrate. In brief, every ten households were to be grouped together under a headman; ten such groupings constituted a chia, again with a headman; and each ten chia formed a pao, under a pao headman. These decimal groupings of 100 households into a chia and 1,000 households into a pao were deliberately not intended to correspond with the rural villages and the townships (hsiang) which were the natural divisions in rural China. In practice, however, it proved impossible to maintain the distinction, just as it was impossible to expect that the nongentry headmen would be able to carry out their police functions against the interests of the local elite. There was thus, and especially in the nineteenth century, a tendency for the pao-chia system to be absorbed into the local society and for the local gentry to exercise an increasing formal or informal role--both tendencies which subverted the original purposes of the institu-tion.

The li-chia institutions were never even in theory as uniformly implemented as the pao-chia. Its decimal groupings were similar to but legally distinct from the surveillance system: 110 households made up a li, with the ten wealthiest among them providing the li headmen; the remaining 100 households were divided into groups of ten called chia, again under headmen. The original function of the chia head was to collect the tax records of the families under him and give them to the li headman, who in turn forwarded them to the magistrate's yamen (office). Even by the eighteenth century the li-chia system had considerably atrophied. It rapidly evolved from an institution for registering tax-paying households--to facilitate the state's collection of all the revenue that was legally due it--into one which participated in the actual collection of taxes--in the in-terest of influential members of the gentry who paid at lower rates and of yamen underlings who profited from illegal extra exactions and from "deals" with the favored gentry.

Manchuria, Mongolia, Turkestan, and Tibet

Of the three Manchurian provinces of Fengtien, Kirin, and Heilungkiang, large parts of Fengtien (present day Liaoning), the southernmost, had even in the Ming been economically and politically incorporated into the Chinese cultural sphere. During the Ch'ing, until the major reorganization of Manchuria toward the end of the dynasty, Fengtien was governed approximately as a province of China proper--although its situation was complicated until 1876 by a division of authority between the military governor and a regional government with its Five Boards (all except Civil Appointments) in the Manchu auxiliary capital of Sheng-ching (Mukden, Shen-yang in the Ming). Kirin in central Manchuria and Heilungkiang on the northern frontier were, however, organized on a purely military basis. This distinction reflected a determined Ch'ing policy to preserve political control of the nonsinicized parts of their homeland exclusively in Manchu hands and to minimize cultural contacts with China proper. Chinese immigration into Kirin and Heilungkiang was prohibited and the adoption of Chinese cultural traits was discouraged. Insofar as this policy was motivated by a desire to preserve the fountainhead of Manchu ancestral virtues and to maintain a reservoir of Central Asian-type military power such as that which had conquered the Ming, its import was more emotional than political. The basic political reason for opposing acculturating influences was a fear that if the traditional social system in these tribal areas and in adjacent Mongolia were undermined, this might lead to a repetition of the process whereby the Manchus themselves under Nurhaci had become sinified enough to conquer and rule China.

Separate military rule of northern Manchuria by units of the banner forces was, however, gradually undermined because (1) it was a strategic area facing Russia and Mongolia whose defenses would be strengthened by Chinese exiles and convicts and later by immigrants; (2) it was impossible to prevent illegal Chinese immigration into the largely virgin land from the crowded districts of north China; and (3) the sinicized Peking Manchus who usually headed the military administration themselves were instrumental in importing Chinese culture. In the post-Taiping period, and especially after 1895, rapid steps were belatedly taken to reverse the separatist policy, to encourage Chinese immigration, and to institute Chinese-type provincial administration.

I shall discuss the incorporation of Mongolia, Turkestan, and Tibet into the Ch'ing empire in another essay. Here I want only to note that these areas during most of the dynasty were governed largely as colonial possessions. They were under the jurisdiction of the Superintendency of Dependencies (Li-fan yuan) which the Manchus had first established in Mukden in 1638 to control the Inner Mongol tribes who had been defeated and enlisted in the Manchu banner system. The organization and status of the Li-fan yuan in the Peking government were roughly the same as one of the Six Boards, except that it had only one president and one vice-president. These officials were usually Manchus, before the Ch'ien-lung reign occasionally Mongols, but never Chinese. Ch'ing relations with Russia were also handled through the Li-fan yuan.

Military Organization

Prior to the middle of the nineteenth century, the armed forces of the Ch'ing empire consisted of two components: the banner system, whose origins I described earlier, and the "Army of the Green Standard" (Lü-ying), a force developed from the remnants of the Ming military system. The banners--which had been the main striking force in the conquest of China--were by the eighteenth century largely garrison troops protecting strategic points, while the Green Standard troops were employed, together with some banner troops, in the extensive Central Asian campaigns of the K'ang-hsi and Ch'ien-lung emperors, and were primarily responsible for maintaining internal order.

Considerable uncertainty remains about the exact size of the banner forces, probably arising from the difficulty of distinguishing between "able-bodied men" liable for military duty and the number who were actually mobilized as soldiers. As I have already noted, the banners were comprehensive organizations which enrolled the entire Manchu population as well as early Chinese and Mongol adherents to the Manchu cause. At the time of the conquest in 1644, there were 278 Manchu companies (niru), 120 Mongol and 165 Chinese. The number of warriors in each niru was fixed at about 200 in 1634. If we assume one able-bodied male per family and an average family size of six persons--which is probably low as the Manchu extended family tended to be larger than the Chinese average--it may be roughly estimated that the total population of China's conquerors was 675,600, of whom 112,600 were soldiers.

The number of companies increased with the growth of population over the next century, but the quota of fighting men per <u>niru</u> fell as low as 100. During the Ch'ien-lung reign about 100,000 banner troops and their families, representing 681 Manchu, 204 Mongol, and 266 Chinese <u>niru</u>, were quartered in Peking and provided the main force defending the emperor and the capital. One hundred thousand more, organized in 840 <u>niru</u>, were garrisoned in the provinces and on the frontiers. The total banner population, soldiers and dependents, was thus about 1,200,000 in the mid-eighteenth century.

In Peking, the bannermen resided primarily in the "Tartar City" section of the capital, separated by walls from the "Chinese City." The provincial garrisons included 26 small posts (about 10,000 troops) in the metropolitan province of Chihli which protected the approaches to the capital; at least 36,000 troops in Manchuria divided among 43 scattered posts in the frontier areas and 20 posts in Liaotung; 12,000-15,000 troops in six posts in Chinese Turkestan --to guard against incursions from the north and west; and 45,000-50,000 troops stationed at about 20 strategic locations in eleven of the provinces of China proper. These last were concentrated in major population centers, e.g., Nanking, Hangchow, Foochow, Chengtu, and Canton, and at critical points like Chinkiang where the Grand Canal intersects the Yangtze river. The numbers given above varied in the course of the dynasty, but the proportions in the three main sectors remained about the same. As in Peking, the banner troops and their families in the provinces resided in fortified quarters segregated from the Chinese population of the garrison cities and were not under the jurisdiction of the local civil officials.

The general headquarters of the Peking banners was staffed by a lieutenant-general (<u>tu-t'ung</u>) and his subordinates. In each of the garrisoned provinces, the banner forces were commanded by a general (<u>chiang-chün</u>, referred to as the "Tartar General" by foreigners in the nineteenth century) and two brigade-generals (<u>fu tu-t'ung</u>), all of whom were Manchus. As the provincial garrisons were widely separated and not usually larger than 4,000 men, once the conquest had been completed the Ch'ing clearly did not depend entirely upon dynastic military power to maintain its control over China proper. Civil government and the Green Standard battalions in a pinch were more important.

During the first years of the dynasty, especially in north China, substantial amounts of land and buildings (but never more than a few percent of the total land acreage in China) were expropriated from Chinese owners to support the conquering banner forces. While large imperial estates and holdings by Manchu nobles and officers continued until 1911 (and after, in the case of the imperial household), such allotments as were given to individual bannermen were quickly lost by mortgage or (illegal) sale to the more enterprising Chinese population. From 1656 bannermen and their families were supported by cash stipends paid from the government's tax revenue. These payments, however, fell behind their natural population growth and the price inflation of the eighteenth century. Relative poverty, coupled with the inaction of garrison life and a context of apparently increasing corruption, by the Ch'ien-lung reign at least had severely reduced the military effectiveness of the banner forces in China proper. While the banner system succeeded in perpetuating a hereditary military caste which served implicitly as an arm of the dynasty itself, from the beginning of the eighteenth century until the middle of the nineteenth, the real military power--"the regular army"-- of the Ch'ing empire consisted of the professional Chinese soldiers of the Army of the Green Standard.

The Green Standard troops--so named in the same manner as the banners were distinguished by their yellow, white, red and blue flags--were prominently employed by the K'ang-hsi emperor in the suppression of the Rebellion of the Three Feudatories. The eighteenth century conquest of Central Asia was accomplished with mixed armies commanded by Manchu generals and consisting of Green Standard forces and smaller banner contingents. When not engaged in campaigns, the Lü-ying, like the Ming army upon which it was modelled, was a garrison army made up of Chinese soldiers often recruited from families who had served in the army for generations, and of Chinese and Manchu officers who qualified for their bureaucratic posts by military examinations. While officers were regularly transferred from unit to unit by the Board of War, the ordinary soldier was permanently attached to a garrison post--usually in the region of which he was a native--to which he returned when a campaign was completed.

Although they were successfully employed in the dynasty's Central Asian campaigns and against border uprisings, this was the only significant fighting which the Green Standard units saw. During the eighteenth century the Ch'ing experienced a long period of internal peace and was not, except in Central Asia, threatened on its borders. The principal responsibility of the Lü-ying troops was to serve as a local constabulary. They were--as a consequence of a deliberate policy to prevent any concentration of provincial military power that might threaten the dynasty--so organized that effective mobilization against any really large-scale internal or external enemies was extremely difficult. The governors-general and governors, as ex-officio presidents and vice-presidents of the Board of War, nominally commanded all the Green Standard troops in their jurisdictions. They had direct control, however, only over relatively small brigades. Even the provincial commander-in-chief (t'i-tu) directly commanded only a somewhat larger brigade. The bulk of the provincial troops were under the command of semi-independent brigade-generals (tsung-ping)--two or more to a province, 66 in all of China proper--but these forces were scattered in small garrisons throughout the province. Each of these interests --and the Board of War which appointed, promoted, transferred, and disciplined the officer corps--served as a check on the employment of the army by the others. Local officials were opposed to any concentration of troops that would strip their localities of constabulary and undermine the maintenance of order for which they were responsible. None of the commanders from the t'i-tu down could move troops without the approval of the governor-general or governor. These high officials, even when they could get cooperation from the military commanders, were permitted to use their troops only within the borders of their provinces. When faced with serious uprisings or border threats, the dynasty normally appointed a special imperial commissioner to command troops drawn from several garrisons in one or more provinces.

The statutory number of Green Standard troops varied in the course of the dynasty, but we may take it as approximately 500,000 to 600,000. From the end of the eighteenth century there began to be a substantial gap between this quota and the smaller number of actual soldiers, a sign that these forces, like the banners, were in decline. Officers did not seriously attempt to impede desertions, as they could continue to pocket the rations and wages of the absent men. Garrison life undermined discipline and military skills. Training was neglected or at most became a quaint formality. Weapons were largely unchanged from what they had been at the beginning of the dynasty.

In the case of its armed services at least, the Ch'ing was
almost too successful in the first century and a half of its rule.
The decentralized banner and Green Standard battalions had been
sufficient to maintain internal order and to guard or expand the
northern and western frontiers from which in the past all external
threats had come.   But apart from the period of conquest and consolidation, the demands on the military for either purpose had not
been heavy.   In an ideological context in which in any case the
martial virtues were subordinated to the Confucian extolment of
civil rule, the banners and the Army of the Green Standard, although
they continued to consume a large proportion of the imperial revenue
were permitted to decay.   Neither would be effective against the
higher level of social dissidence or the qualitatively different external
challenge which faced the dynasty in the nineteenth century.

The Process of Central Government

In form, and very often in content, administrative actions by
the Ch'ing government were usually initiated by its high officials in
the capital and in the provinces rather than by the emperor.   Especially in the nineteenth century, but also earlier, the more important
business most frequently originated with the "line" agencies in the
provinces rather than the "staff" offices in Peking.   Communication
between officials in either location and the emperor was conducted
by means of "memorials" to the throne on the one hand and imperial
"endorsements," "rescripts," or "edicts" in reply.   Memorials from
the provinces and the offices in the capital were of two main types
--routine and important--and were handled in quite different ways.
The routine memorials were those designated t'i-pen, which generally
concerned local civil affairs and were or became public documents
--in the sense that they passed through so many hands that their
contents frequently became widely known.   If they originated in the
provinces, on arrival in Peking they were examined for form by
the Transmission Office and then forwarded to the Grand Secretariat;
metropolitan officials submitted their t'i-pen directly to the Grand
Secretariat.   In the office of the Secretariat a memorial was first
read by junior officials who drafted one or more suggestions for the
imperial reply.   The memorials and the draft replies in Chinese and
Manchu were then considered by the grand secretaries who approved,
rejected, or amended the drafts, and on the following day at a dawn
audience presented the documents to the emperor who indicated his
decision on the matter in question.   The imperial decision could

take the form of an endorsement, such as a laconic "noted," or a longer rescript might be appended to the document itself. If a separate imperial edict were called for, which was not often the case with the routine t'i-pen, the Grand Council would usually be responsible for drafting it. Appropriate copies were made in Chinese and Manchu as the regulations required--for example, for the historical archives--and the memorialist and others concerned were informed of the imperial decision so that they might act accordingly. Given the large number of such routine memorials, it is unlikely that any one received more than cursory attention from the ruler, although he was indeed expected to see them all.

From the beginning of the eighteenth century, important matters of state (and the personal affairs of the memorialists) began to be communicated via a different type of memorial designated tsou-pen (or tsou-che from 1747). This procedure originated in the efforts of the K'ang-hsi emperor in the 1690s to obtain accurate private information from the provinces by requesting Chinese "bondservants" (early adherents to the Manchu cause who had been absorbed into the Manchu banner system) whom he particularly trusted to submit periodic secret reports directly to the throne. In the early eighteenth century this privilege was extended first to the top regular provincial officials and then to incumbents of the important capital offices as well. The development of the secret memorial system coincided with the efforts of K'ang-hsi and Yung-cheng to reduce the influence of the Manchu princes on the one hand and to secure firm control over the bureaucracy on the other. Handling the flow of tsou-che and the imperial replies thereto--i.e., nonroutine affairs --became the responsibility of the Grand Council, which was thus in a position to advise the throne on the more important political decisions which had to be made. As one or more of the four grand secretaries, two Manchus and two Chinese, and two assistant grand secretaries, one Manchu and one Chinese, was usually a grand councillor as well, there was a direct link between these two bodies, but it was procedurally and substantively very clear that the Grand Secretariat's responsiblity did not extend beyond routine matters.

Important memorials from the provinces and the capital offices were delivered directly to an imperial palace agency called the Chancery of Memorials to the Emperor. They arrived in special sealed dispatch boxes and were forwarded by the Chancery directly to the emperor, who read them and noted his decision with a simple endorsement or indicated that he would like the Grand Council to draft a more elaborate response. For a memorial which required further consideration, the councillors or their subordinates, the secretaries of the Grand Council, prepared drafts--endorsements, rescripts, or edicts--of imperial replies. At the dawn audience on the following day, the emperor and the councillors considered the draft replies in a relatively informal session. When the imperial decision had been made, copies of the memorial and the imperial response were made by the Grand Council and transmitted to the appropriate officials for action. Separate edicts might be issued to the Grand Council or Grand Secretariat or embodied in court letters (t'ing-chi) to the high provincial officials. Many but not all of the tsou-che and the imperial replies thereto were secret; in practice, the emperor had considerable leeway along the spectrum from secret through semisecret to open communications with his officials. The number of tsou-che received daily was considerably less than the numerous t'i-pen; this, together with the secretness and relative informality of their consideration by the ruler and grand councillors, insured that the more urgent matters of state usually received careful attention.

With this description of the flow of business to and from the person of the emperor as a basis, a number of observations about the operations of the Ch'ing central government might be made. As I have already stated, imperial actions on important matters were simultaneously executive decisions and acts of legislation. The emperor's rescripts in some cases, but especially his edicts --which were separate and distinct documents--formed the chief body of law in the empire. They were most importantly codified in the several editions of the Ta-Ch'ing Hui-tien which I have described earlier. Or imperial legislation might take the form of a classified selection of edicts, for example the Yung-cheng emperor's Shih-tsung sheng-hsün [Sacred instructions of the Emperor Shih-tsung, 1741] or the more comprehensive Shih-ch'ao sheng-hsün [Sacred instructions of ten reigns, 1880]. The Six Boards and other agencies compiled and published from time to time collections of regulations relevant to their several responsibilities, in each instance based on memorials presented to the throne and the emperor's responses thereto. And even the administrative manuals and other legal compilations by provincial officials or specialized agencies such as the salt monopoly, which comprised executive decisions by high bureaucrats rather than the emperor, were ultimately only explications of prior imperial decisions. In sum, a very large body of precedents was built up, in theory none that came later violating what the imperial ancestors had decreed. The force of precedent was certainly strong, but the evidence of the compilations themselves suggests that their very bulk and the sometimes ad hoc process of decision-making provided room for some flexibility within an unaltered ideological and institutional framework.

The judicial interpretation of the law was also ultimately performed by the emperor through the same process of memorials and imperial responses which established the legislation in question. Substantively the Ch'ing laws may be divided into three categories: penal laws which specified sanctions for criminal acts; laws on administrative punishment which applied to officials and specified noncriminal sanctions such as demotion for administrative derelections; and administrative regulations which established the positive requirements for bureaucratic performance but specified no sanctions. The Ta-Ch'ing lü-li [Statutes and substatutes of the Great Ch'ing] of 1740 remained the standard codification of the penal laws until the extensive legal reforms of the last years of the dynasty. Revision, addition, or exclusion of substatutes was, however, undertaken every few years until 1863.

Cases under the penal law in the first instance were tried by the local magistrate, who could pronounce and execute sentence only in minor cases, that is, if the penalty were no more than beating. In all more serious cases the magistrate could make only provisional findings and refer the cases to the prefect who in turn transmitted them to the provincial judicial commissioner (an-ch'a shih). Judgments made by the judicial commissioner required the concurrence of the governor and governor-general. Cases of homicide and those in which the possible punishment was more severe than imprisonment were required to be referred by the province to the Board of Punishments which exercised final jurisdiction in all matters except cases punishable by death. These were decided by a body known collectively as the Three High Courts (the Grand Court of Revision, and representatives from the Censorate and the Board of Punishments), but their judgment had to be ratified by the emperor personally.

Once made known, it was expected that the emperor's will

would be carried out by the subordinates to whom it was directed. But the question immediately arises of how the ruler could insure that he was accurately informed of the actions of the bureaucracy, and himself had adequate information upon which to base his decisions. The memorial system itself, especially the tsou-che which gave the memorialists the opportunity for relatively informal reports to the ruler, was an important part of the imperial communications network. There were many inducements for officials to report not only on matters under their own direct responsibility but also on the activities of their colleagues. In the provinces, for example, the emperor could expect that the fact that each reported to the throne directly would serve as some check on the governor-general and governor in a particular locality. And while this became more circumscribed in the latter part of the eighteenth century, the financial commissioners and provincial judges at times were also able to memorialize directly without going through their superiors. To facilitate communications between the provinces and the capital, the Board of War supervised a wide network of over 2,000 postal stations for the transfer of documents by horse, cart or boat (and for the travel of bureaucrats in their official capacity). These stations were supported locally from the land tax revenue. Access to their facilities was controlled by the issuance of tallies to the couriers or travellers which allowed them to claim horses and supplies along their routes. Dispatches carried on horseback from Canton to Peking, for example, (ca. 1,800 miles) were expected to arrive in 32 days, although in the case of urgency the time might be cut in half. From Nanking to Peking (ca. 800 miles), the normal time limit was 13 days.

To some degree the Censorate provided a separate channel for imperial access to information. Its decided conservatism, especially in the latter part of the dynasty, tended however to direct its attention more to matters of form and the minutiae of administration than to policy matters. Memorials from provincial officials were frequently referred to one or more of the Six Boards for comment before an imperial decision. While the Boards, too, were rarely imaginative and often tied up in their own precedents, they were sometimes headed by individuals with substantial competence who could provide useful staff papers. The emperor, through the regular audiences which all officials were expected to receive before assuming office, had at least the possibility of personally questioning a wide spectrum of bureaucrats about their opinions and experiences.

It was his practice also to dispatch special imperial commissioners
to the provinces from time to time to investigate matters of particular concern, or to take charge of situations that had gotten out
of hand. And the K'ang-hsi and Ch'ien-lung emperors, as I have
noted, each personally toured the southern provinces on six occasions.

Yet the problem remained that the emperor, in spite of these
multiple channels of information, might be isolated--cut off in his
palace from the realities of his empire. Given the fact that the
flow of official business all ultimately ended on his desk, so to
speak, that he had to rule as well as reign if the political system
were to function, only an extraordinary man could cope with his
enormous responsibilities. It made a difference who sat on the
throne, and with all the flexibility that Ch'ing practice for the selection of the monarch permitted, there was never a guarantee that
the right choice would be made. And what made a difference, too,
was the morale of the bureaucracy. Imperial incompetence or
excessive arbitrariness could not be prevented by the bureaucracy,
but its consequences could be avoided in part by a withdrawal into
passivity or into implicit collusion which sought mutual protection
by withholding from the throne any disquieting information. In a
sense this was the proud Confucian official's unspoken dissent from
a government in which the right principles did not prevail. The
same official demoralization might result from circumstances outside of imperial control--as, for example, from new levels of
internal dissidence or unprecedented external threats with which
the traditional political system, irrespective of the quality of the
ruler, could not cope in its accustomed ways. When we look at
the nineteenth century, we can, I suggest, quite legitimately discern
a cumulative decline in morale, a shattering of the shining eighteenth-century self-image, a progressive loss of the psychological
Mandate of Heaven--now not just by the monarch, but jointly by
emperor and officials together.

The Process of Local Government

The omnipotence--which really meant the total responsibility--
of the emperor in the affairs of his realm was mirrored some 1,500
times in the smaller realms of the department and district magistrates who were his agents for local government. Administration
by higher provincial officials and by the capital offices consisted

largely of the movement of paper; it was at the level of the magistrate's _yamen_ (government office) that the imperial state directly confronted the population of the empire. And this was the principal locus, too, of the interplay between formal and informal government which I suggested earlier helps to account for the remarkable longevity and stability of the traditional Chinese political system.

While the Ch'ing regulations provided for a number of categories of minor officials subordinate to the magistrates, fewer than half of the _chou_ and fewer than a third of the _hsien_ had assistant magistrates. In any case, neither these nor other subordinates were authorized to act independently of the magistrate, who was expected personally to take charge of all judicial cases (except minor civil disputes) in his district and to count and arrange for the forwarding of tax receipts to the provincial treasurer. These two functions--the maintenance of order, including the administration of justice, and the collection of tax quotas were the principal content of government at the local level, and the magistrate was held accountable for their performance when his service record was examined by the Boards of Civil Appointments at the expiration of his normal three-year term of office. More than 90 percent of the local magistrates in the Ch'ing period were ethnic Chinese. About three-quarters of the _hsien_ and 40 percent of the _chou_ magistrates were holders of the _chin-shih_ or _chü-jen_ degrees--among the rest a significant proportion (13 percent and 28 percent for the _hsien_ and _chou_ respectively) had qualified for office by purchasing a _chien-sheng_ title. By regulation, a magistrate was not permitted to hold office in his native province or in a neighboring province within 160 miles (500 _li_) of his home district.

General administrator, judge, tax collector--these roles were performed within the magistrate's offices (_yamen_) which were usually located in the principal walled city in his district. The daily _yamen_ schedule began with the magistrate holding his "morning court" at which he conferred with his subordinates, received and dispatched documents, questioned prisoners, and (on certain designated days) received complaints from the populace. Lawsuits, which occupied a major part of his time, were heard in the afternoon and sometimes in the evening as well. During the period when land taxes were being collected, the magistrate conducted hearings to discipline laggard taxpayers and ineffective collectors. A good deal of his time was also consumed in drafting and reading documents, and some in ritual responsibilities such as regular visits to the local Confucian temple and the temple of the city god.

The magistrate's statutory salary, like that of all other officials, was very low--from 45 to 80 taels (ounces of silver) per annum. From the Yung-cheng reign onward, officials received in addition to their nominal stipends more substantial supplementary allowances which were termed yang-lien yin (literally, "money to nourish honesty"). For the magistrates these ranged from 400 to 2,250 taels annually depending on the locality. A small office allowance of 500 to 700 taels was also provided. His private and official expenses, however, exceeded this regular income several times over. In addition to the ordinary personal expenses of maintaining his family, a magistrate paid the salaries of his private secretaries, was expected to make "contributions" to the provincial treasurer as needed, had to entertain and provide gifts for his superior officials and visiting dignitaries, and was obliged to pay substantial "customary fees" to the personnel of superior offices in order to transact business with them without obstruction. The more general point to be made here is that local government in China had no independent regular revenues of its own; all taxes were levied by the central government and had to be remitted in full in accordance with the established quotas. Local government--the hsien magistrate's expenses and the sustenance of his numerous underlings, as well as similar outlays at higher levels of the provincial hierarchy--was financed primarily by the collection of "customary fees" (lou-kuei, literally "base custom") from the population of the departments and districts. These were, as the colloquial term for them suggests, irregular levies, in the sense that they were neither specifically authorized by imperial edict nor uniform from locality to locality. But they were not illegal, because in theory at least they were fees for official services. While in practice the line is hard to draw, lou-kuei should be distinguished from official "corruption" which I shall discuss later.

Of the many different kinds of customary fees, some of the more common were: a meltage fee to compensate for the silver lost in the process of casting the smaller pieces received as taxes into standard ingots (in 1724 this was regularized by the central government and allocated to provide the "money to nourish honesty" mentioned above); the collection of copper coins as tax payments in lieu of silver at an exchange rate higher than the market; the assessment of extra allowances of rice to compensate for wastage in storage and transit from those who paid rice tribute; "gifts" to newly appointed magistrates from clerks and runners; fees for pao-chia door placards, tax assessment notices, and land surveys; payments for the acceptance and processing of legal cases; license fees; fees for the transfer of property; and the purchase of supplies for the yamen at "official" prices. These payments either went directly to the magistrate, or were made to his clerks, runners, and servants, or in some cases were shared by the official and his subordinates. What they had in common is that they were acknowledged as customary and thus legitimate by the populace; what went beyond custom was corruption, and was strongly if not effectively resisted.

There may appear to be a contradiction between the references just made to numerous underlings and the statement that the chou and hsien magistrates were the lowest officials in the hierarchy of imperial government. The latter implies that China was only superficially governed at the local level, while the former suggests a plenitude of attention. What I mean to suggest is not that there was no "government" in Chinese society below the district level, but rather that imperial control of that "government" through the person of the magistrate was indeed often superficial. His responsibilities were all-encompassing, but his omnipotence was only theoretical. Even more than his sovereign whose relations with his official servants--the bureaucracy--were sometimes ambiguous, the magistrate--by law a stranger in the district he was sent to govern, and a short-term resident too--could be a captive of local interests rather than their master.

At times the magistrate might not even know the local dialect. He certainly was not familiar with local problems and rarely had time in the usual three-year incumbency to overcome that handicap. To meet the tax quotas, to maintain order, to adjudicate the civil and criminal cases presented to him, to handle the enormous quantity of paperwork which the administrative code required in the exercise of these functions--to do his job well, he was dependent both on the day-to-day functioning of numerous clerks, messengers, guards, doormen, police, and servants and on the goodwill and cooperation of the local elite. Only to a limited extent could he and his personal servants and advisers understand or control the local interests, which might themselves be in collusion, represented by those two groups of permanent residents of his district.

The magistrate's yamen staff consisted of four categories of personnel. Responsibility for drafting correspondence, preparing routine reports and memoranda, maintaining the files, issuing warrants, and the like was assigned to a body of clerks (li or shu-li) who were natives of the district and according to a frequently violated statute were limited to five-year terms. They might in practice number from 200 to 2,000 per district, although the official quota was usually much smaller. The clerks of necessity were literate in some degree, and were permitted to take examinations that might qualify them as rank 9b officials after five years in office. As no salaries were paid to them, their acknowledged income consisted entirely of customary fees (to which the profits of corruption might be added). Because they were natives, often outlasted any particular magistrates, were familiar with the precedents of the office, and handled most of its documents, their opportunities for corruption--in the form either of extortions from the peasantry or collaboration with the local elite--were great. While the administrative code held the magistrate strictly responsible for the malfeasances of his yamen clerks, he ordinarily found it difficult to control them.

Under the general heading of "runners" (ya-i), the second category, were included several hundred to several thousand messengers, police, guards, servants, doormen, lictors, janitors, etc. Like the clerks they were local men, and while they were paid small salaries, the runners too were primarily dependent upon lou-kuei for their sustenance. And also like the yamen clerks, with whom they sometimes cooperated, they had frequent opportunities to supplement their incomes through bribery and extortion--as the initial investigators of homicides and other crimes, and as messengers to the rural areas to press for the payment of the land tax, for example. The legal and social status of the runners was considerably lower than that of the clerks, but their connection with the magistrate's office was sufficient to make the general population wary of them. Again, the transient magistrate could not always control them.

The third and fourth categories of yamen personnel were, unlike the clerks and runners, few in number, not natives of the district, and personal employees of the magistrate rather than of the government. Perhaps twenty or so personal servants (ch'ang-sui) were brought with him by a magistrate when he arrived at a new post. A few were cooks and the like, but most were used by the magistrate as part of his office staff to supervise the clerks, manage the flow of persons and documents, check tax records and collections, and oversee the procedure at trials--all in the interest of increasing the magistrate's control over the yamen clerks and runners. These personal servants received wages from the magistrate, but they were small enough so that they too were dependent on the proceeds of customary fees. In view of their sharing this common interest with the clerks and runners whom they were supposed to supervise, it is perhaps not surprising that the desire for personal gain sometimes overrode their commitment to the magistrate's cause.

Only the magistrate's private secretaries (mu-yu), who received adequate salaries from their employer, did not normally participate in the system of lou-kuei. These advisers may be described as experts in administration who were engaged by the magistrate because they had acquired special competence in one or more of such fields as law, taxation, or accounting. Many of them were holders of the lowest examination degree, which did not qualify them for office, and had hopes at least of becoming officials themselves. Given the situation that the magistrate was most often a Confucian "generalist," his effective handling of his two major responsibilities of taxation and justice depended heavily upon the skills of his mu-yu. And as scholars themselves, indoctrinated in the Confucian values, they could be expected to support a magistrate who took seriously the moral responsibilities of office.

In operation these institutions were characterized by a continuing tension between the magistrate, seconded by his mu-yu, who was expected to carry out in a universalistic manner the detailed prescriptions and prohibitions of the imperial administrative code, and the yamen underlings who were deeply imbedded in a local context where personal ties and diffuse rather than specific actions were the norms of conduct. As the magistrate, too, was in part dependent upon informal income from lou-kuei, the center of gravity of local government was not unexpectedly less often in the bureaucratic sphere which the imperial regulations described than in the customary nexuses of the local society upon which it was superimposed. Although there were many honorable exceptions, the modal magistrate tended to be a passive governor who was satisfied with being able to forward the taxes assessed against his district and to maintain a semblance of order. The relations between the populace and the yamen personnel continued in established and informal channels as magistrate succeeded magistrate, to the benefit not only of the clerks and runners but also of the local elite whose relationship with the emperor's bureaucratic outpost in the district yamen was also an ambiguous one.

On the positive side, in the matter of prevention of local disorder, was the gentry's assumption of leadership responsibilities in a number of areas that we would consider quasi-governmental; arbitration of disputes, public works, education, welfare and relief, and local defense are examples. Access to the magistrate on terms of equality by gentry with high status could sometimes benefit the entire populace of the locality, for example, by initiating a tax deferral or reduction in the event of severe flooding or drought. On the other hand, the local elite were at least as much concerned with protecting and enhancing their own class interests as with the general welfare. Among the variety of means to this end, the following were common: payment of de facto lower rates of taxation by escaping some of the surcharges to which nongentry landowners were subjected; gentry households undertaking to pay taxes at their own lower rates on behalf of commoner landowners in return for a commission; and interference in the administration of justice in the interest of their lineages or families. Practices of this sort required either sufficient status to overawe the magistrate or some quid pro quo to the yamen staff. But such conflicts of interest as there were between the local elite and the yamen were never serious enough to undermine their joint interest in maintaining a social system in which officials and gentry were both part of the same ruling class.

Politics: Who Gets What, When, How

As a result of its legislative, executive, and judicial actions, a government would expect to accomplish certain ends, among them: to remain in power, to defend state and society against external enemies, to suppress internal rebellion, to maintain the social order, and to affect the economy. I have treated the phenomenon of domestic rebellion in China in another place, and the remaining sections of the present essay consider the economy and society. With apologies to Professor Lasswell, here I shall take up briefly several matters related to "remaining in power" that the previous discussion in this section has already implicitly touched upon. Three questions require further comment: Who was in power--did the Ch'ing political system operate exclusively in the interests of the Manchu

minority? How was that power exercised--was it despotic? milita-
tistic? And third, was political power in Ch'ing China particularly
susceptible to "corruption"? One does not have to look very hard
to become aware of an historiography which dismisses the whole
Ch'ing period as a corrupt and despotic Manchu dictatorship over
the Chinese people. Was it so?

I prefer an alternative formulation which acknowledges a distinct Manchu interest in the Ch'ing polity, but also recognizes that
it was much more diffuse than and did not at all neatly correspond
to either the dynasty (i.e., the interests of the emperor) or the
state (emperor and bureaucracy). By becoming emperors of China,
the Manchu leaders in effect had already abandoned any simple commitment to serving Manchu parochial interests. The Chinese monarchy, in the definition which the Ch'ing emperors also accepted, was
a universal one for which the ruler's qualifications were moral and
cultural rather than ethnic. Having assumed Heaven's Mandate--
albeit by force of arms--the monarch could sustain his power only
by governing in the interests of the whole of the political and social
elite whose ideology defined his authority and who carried his writ
into practice. Possibly the Ch'ing efforts to maintain Manchuria as
a nonsinified cultural preserve, to prohibit intermarriage with Han
Chinese, and to keep the Manchu language in use at least in court
documents were in the early years of the dynasty actually intended
to provide the organizational and physical basis for a continuous
renewal of the "Central Asian" military power with which China had
been conquered. It is, however, difficult to accept that after the
seventeenth century these were more than symbolic gestures; no
men--not even "barbarians" in the advanced stages of acculturation
--easily abandon the emotional tug of their past. The Yung-cheng
emperor should, I believe, be taken as expressing his true inten-
tions if not always his practice when he claimed to "make no distinction between Manchus and Chinese, but preserve only the most
scrupulous impartiality toward all my subjects." Although the emperor was a Manchu, his imperial interest was ultimately neither
Chinese nor Manchu--it was the preservation of his rule.

For the dynasty, given its origins, there was a great pull
toward "Chineseness" in form and content as a guarantee, so to
speak, of its legitimacy. I have noted that the Literary Inquisition
of the Ch'ien-lung period was particularly concerned to censor any
unflattering references to the Ch'ing's "barbarian" origins. Even

more than if they had been ethnic Chinese, the Ch'ing emperors
were impelled to restore and uphold the mainstream of Confucian
orthodoxy as exemplified in the publication and dissemination under
imperial auspices of the writings of the Chu Hsi school. Not only
were the Manchu imperial clan, nobility, and officials increasingly
sinicized, but the basic institutions which we identify with the Chinese social order--the landholding system and the structure of local
society, qualification for public office primarily through government
examinations, and the constitution of government itself--were retained
largely intact. The employment of Manchu officials in a ratio greatly
out of proportion to their number in the population of the empire
was not simply because they were ethnically Manchu, but at least
as importantly because they could be counted upon to support loyally
the interests of the emperor qua emperor--as also could the Chinese
bannermen who held most of the top provincial posts in the seventeenth century. An ethnic Chinese emperor also placed his long-
tested supporters in office, in preference to the sometime followers
of his rivals. Major political divisions after the first decades of
the dynasty and before the end of the nineteenth century were not
usually along Chinese-Manchu lines. For two hundred years few
Chinese intellectuals or officials were troubled--though some res-
torationist secret societies might have been--by the "Manchu question." And even in the republican revolutionary movement after
1895, there was more than a hint of opportunism in the employment
of an anti-Manchu racist theme.

In sum, I am not convinced that in the eighteenth and most of
the nineteenth centuries it made any great difference that the ruling
house was not Han Chinese. There is little reason to believe that
the great rebellions would not have occurred or that the foreigners'
demands would have been withstood any more strongly if the dynasty
had been established by domestic rebels--as in the case of the Ming
--rather than by semiacculturated "barbarian" conquerors. But if
the Ch'ing was not just a closed Manchu holding company, was it
not still despotic--even more so than Chinese dynasties had been?
If the emperor's interest was only to retain and enjoy his power,
then because he was a Manchu and not a Chinese was not that power
more vulnerable, and was he not therefore compelled to act more
arbitrarily in order to keep it?

Some nationalist historians have made a point of comparing
Ch'ing political institutions with those of the Ming and finding the

former, like other "barbarian" regimes, an examplar of despotic
tribal political power. Their argument goes like this: the Ch'ing
went along with the Ming abolition of the office of prime minister
which had been the command post of bureaucratic power in the state
as against that of the emperor. But in establishing the Grand Council it proceeded even further down the road of concentrating power
in the hands of the monarch--by substituting secret personal contact
between the emperor and his officials for the open conduct of administration through the publication of edicts by the Grand Secretariat,
and by increasingly turning the Six Boards into staff rather than
executive offices. The Ch'ing emperors controlled their civil officials and the empire's military forces directly, in contrast to the
Ming when orders were issued only through the presidents of the
Boards of Civil Appointments and War. In the Ming dynasty the
prime minister had designated incumbents of the first four official
ranks and the Board of Civil Appointments had filled ranks five to
nine, but the Ch'ing rulers played a much more direct role in the
selection of officials by appointing to the highest offices directly and
seeing all lower officials in audience before confirming them in their
posts. The Ch'ing provincial administration, too, was more autocratic, with the emperor's direct representatives in the provinces
--the governors-general and governors--now serving as permanent
officials while in the Ming they had been dispatched only on tempo-
rary assignment. In sum, the Manchu emperors reduced the traditional and just (because it was based on Confucian morality) political power of the officials, who were the representatives of the
literati as a whole selected through the examination system. This
they were able to accomplish because they were backed by tribal
military power--the banners, and the Army of the Green Standard
which was also in effect controlled by Manchu officers.

Apart from the quite idealized view of Ming government and
society which the foregoing interpretation presents--political power
as it properly should be was held by the Confucian literati and popular expression of opinion was encouraged: what would the Ming
founder Chu Yuan-chang, or the Yung-lo emperor, or the eunuch
Wei Chung-hsien, or the adherents of the Tung-lin party have thought
of such a formulation!--the issue it seems to me is one of distinguishing form and content. Chinese traditional political institutions
in every dynasty were autocratic, and they might be employed des-
potically by any ruler. No formal institutions per se were ever
much of a check on the tendency of monarchy to enhance its power.

While the Ch'ing modification of the Ming political structure may well have been an even less effective obstruction than the original, the changes made were only minor ones of form; the content of politics remained unaltered. An emperor could be and frequently was despotic in particular cases; the administrative style of the Yung-cheng emperor, with his spy network, his personal humiliation of offending officials, and his authoritarian "Discourse on Parties and Cliques" (P'eng-tang lun, 1725) which denounced official factionalism, was not much of a departure from the practices of the first Ming emperor (Chu Yuan-chang, reigned 1368-1398, temple name T'ai-tsu) and several of his successors. But political power was never rightfully the exclusive possession of either the monarch or his officials. The substance of Chinese traditional politics was that they shared political power but continuously contested with each other over the details of its allocation. Sometimes the balance would shift to one side, sometimes to another. Nothing could bring a dynasty to an end more surely than total imperial despotism against the interests of officialdom and the Confucial elite, even more quickly than increased taxes or brutal conscription of the peasant population. On the other hand, any suggestion that the Ch'ing bureaucracy-- except in its own self-image--was really more just, or moral, or "democratic" than the ruler in relation to the majority nonelite population is ridiculously anachronistic. Emperor and officials together, but not without tension, constituted the imperial state which governed society in such a manner that both were the beneficiaries.

If Ch'ing government was not more--or less--despotic than earlier eras, was it not at least more corrupt and increasingly so? Many descriptions of local government, for example, by nineteenth-century observers and by more recent scholars offer a picture of widespread bribery, extortion, and peculation just beneath the surface of bureaucratic legality. And were not the very large military expenditures of the dynasty more tokens of corruption among both the paymasters in Peking and the field officers than of the actual costs of defeating rather minor enemies? The suppression of uprisings by aborigine tribes in western Szechwan in 1747-1749 and 1771-1776, for example, is said to have required extraordinary military expenditures of 20 million and 70 million taels respectively. Admittedly the terrain along the Golden Sand river was difficult, the climate inhospitable, and the stone tower fortresses of the natives well defended, but the fielding of 40,000 troops in the first instance with only inconclusive results, and 80,000 in the second campaign

against only a few thousand insurgents, was probably also as prof-
itable to the Manchu commanders as it was ultimately disastrous for
the aborigines. And Ho Shen's "profits" from twenty years as the
confidant of the Ch'ien-lung emperor--said to amount to 80,000,000
taels in gold, silver, precious stones, etc.--was not this evidence
that even under the greatest of the Ch'ing emperors corruption had
grown totally out of control?

My view, in brief, is that corruption--the exchange of money
in return for certain types of political conduct (ranging from an
immediate positive benefit to the payee at one end of a spectrum
to the negative act of simply letting him be at the other) in violation
of legal or customary norms--can be found in discernible quantities
in Ch'ing China, that occasionally it occurred on a grand scale, but
that it was not more prevalent than in earlier dynasties. And, moreover, in the short run corruption perhaps performed some positive
functions for those involved which must be weighed against its more
obvious negative effects. When a member of the local elite evaded
some part of the taxes he legally owed, with at least the passive
acquiescence of the magistrate, he was trading his political support
for the difference in silver between what he owed and what he actually paid. If a _yamen_ runner extorted an extra tax surcharge
from a small landowner, it was on the implicit promise that, for
the present, he would demand no more. If an official wanted to
retain his post or get a better one in the years when Ho Shen and
his collaborators were influential in the Board of Civil Appointments,
he resorted to lavish bribes. Peculation by military commanders
from the funds allocated for salaries and supplies might originate
in the need to pay such bribes, or be more simple cases of the
misappropriation of public funds for direct private benefit. The
common characteristic of each of the foregoing examples is that,
unlike the widespread system of customary fees, they were in
violation of accepted norms, and those involved were in theory
liable to some punishment.

But too many persons were involved in such transactions for
the possibility of punishment to be very great. Their participation
was a direct index of the coexistence in the Chinese political system
of the two spheres of political authority which I described earlier
as Level I and Level II. Neither the bureaucratic imperial state
with its universalistic and detailed prescriptions and prohibitions,
nor the competing nexuses of authority rooted in local and particu-

laristic structures (such as community or kinship or common educational experience or patron-client relations) completely dominated the polity. At the interstices where they met, corruption flourished because it could serve as a means of accommodation between the two systems, a means of integrating state and society. Bribery of members of the <u>yamen</u> staff in the hope of influencing a legal case implied an acknowledgement that the imperial state as represented by the magistrate was the proper agent to adjudicate the matter at hand. But it also demonstrated a deliberate insertion into this relatively impersonal proceeding of something more direct and particularistic which was related to the familiar practices of non-bureaucratic local society. The circumstances that <u>yamen</u> clerks and runners were not paid adequate salaries directly by the government demonstrates that they were not fully incorporated into Level I of the polity, although they had to serve it. Their participation in corruption reduced the strain of acting perforce in the interest of the imperial state while sharing few of the values or perquisites of the bureaucrat.

Corruption in imperial China may also be seen as a channel of political influence in a society which had institutionalized only one regular route to political power, that is, promotion from rank to rank in the bureaucratic hierarchy. When a subordinate made substantial "gifts" to his superior--at his own initiative or not--he might be in effect influencing decisions which in other political systems were determined by the public lobbying of organized interest groups. What I am suggesting is not that the costs of corruption were small--ultimately in increased burdens on those at the bottom of the social pyramid as well as in damage to the self-image of official perpetrators--but that to look at it exclusively through the eyes of the Confucian moralist can be misleading. If the practitioners of corruption tried their best to conceal it, its moral critics --whether Confucian contemporaries or latter-day nationalist historians--have equally exaggerated its importance, especially in the case of the Ch'ing dynasty which the historians at least never liked very much. In all periods the Chinese political system, like many others, was to some degree prone to corruption. Some particularly grievous instances are recorded in the Ch'ing period, but they can be matched in other dynasties--or for that matter in republican China. The Ch'ing did not collapse because its government became progressively more corrupt, although in the nineteenth century Manchu rule may for other reasons have become progressively more burdensome materially and psychologically.

IV. ECONOMY AND SOCIETY

The imperial state "governed" an economy and society whose institutions had been established in the T'ang and Sung dynasties (A.D. 618-1278) and underwent few changes of significance before the nineteenth century. Quantity and quality of course varied-- sometimes sharply--but basic modifications in the ways in which China's population produced and consumed the basic necessities of life, and the evolution of the patterns of kinship, social class, and community organization within which they lived had largely been completed centuries before the Manchu conquest. One of the most striking comments that can be made about the Ch'ing conquerors is that they retained pretty much intact the characteristic features of the Chinese social order which they inherited. Indeed, much of what we consider "traditionally Chinese" reached its fullest elaboration during this last of the imperial dynasties.

The Ch'ing Economy

There was little in the Chinese economy prior to the twentieth century that was not included within the agriculture sector or quite intimately connected with it. The emphasis on agriculture in the discussion which follows is thus not without some justification. I shall also consider in turn handicraft industry, commerce, and the relations of the government to the economy. The reader will immediately be aware of the great tentativeness of the occasional quantitative data I cite. In part this reflects the still underdeveloped state of studies of China's economic history; even more it exemplifies the state of the Chinese economy itself which like other premodern fragmented institutions produced little global statistical data for political leaders (and scholars) to manipulate.

From the point of view of the imperial state, the economic system was seen primarily as the producer of the tax revenues which supported the court, the bureaucracy, and the army. Secondarily, its general health was a matter of some concern in the official rhetoric if only because a contented population was not likely to rebel. For the political and social elite, the economy produced the wealth which made possible a comfortable life style and a remarkable high culture; only indirectly, however, before the twentieth century was wealth alone the means to the greatest power and the highest prestige in the society. The bulk of the population expected and received little more than subsistence. The distribution of the current national product rather than its continuous augmentation was the chief interest of each of these constituencies in so far as they thought about economic matters in particular. Growth of aggregate output--though not of per capita output--did take place during the course of the dynasty, but at a declining rate from the end of the eighteenth century when the limitations of available technology and the pressure of population on land began to manifest themselves.

Agriculture

While there were substantial alterations in population size, cultivated acreage, and aggregate output, the technology and organization of Chinese agriculture in the eighteenth century differed little from that of the fourteenth century, and in fact were to remain largely unchanged until the twentieth century. The available official population data are considered relatively reliable for the early Ming and for the period 1776-1851. Together with the 1953 census in the People's Republic of China and an assessment of the demographic effects of the great mid-nineteenth-century rebellions, they provide some benchmarks from which to estimate the gross trend, although not the specific count in any one year, of population changes over some six centuries. Estimates of cultivated acreage can also be derived by adjusting variations in the unit of land measure (mou = roughly one sixth of an acre). Table 4 presents the population and acreage estimates made by one leading student of the Chinese economy which are probably the best reconstructions now available to us.

Unfortunately the seventeenth and early eighteenth century have not yielded enough reliable data for us to attempt to treat the population and acreage trends in the early Ch'ing as a distinct period. We may, however, estimate with some confidence from Table 4 that in the four centuries between 1400 and 1800 the population of China increased by a factor of five or six, while cultivated acreage perhaps tripled. Although population grew at twice the rate of the cultivated acreage, the combination of increased inputs of land, labor, and capital was apparently able, until the beginning of the nineteenth century, to raise the aggregate output of food grains sufficiently to maintain per capita consumption at a minimum customary level. Perhaps one-half of the growth of output was accounted for by the

Table 4

POPULATION AND CULTIVATED ACREAGE ESTIMATES FOR CHINA, 1400-1957
(National Totals, Constant Boundaries)

Year	Population (millions)	Cultivated Acreage (million shih-mou)
1400	65-80	370 (±70)
1600	120-220	500 (±100)
1770	270 (±25)	950 (±100)
1850	410 (±25)	n. a.
1873	350 (±25)	1,210 (±50)
1893	385 (±25)	1,240 (±50)
1913	430 (±25)	1,360 (±50)
1933	500 (±25)	1,470 (±50)
1957	647 (±15)	1,678 (±25)

Source: Dwight H. Perkins, Agriculture Development in China,
1368-1968, Chicago: Aldine, 1969, p. 16, Table II.1.

bringing of new land under cultivation (this in itself required considerable investment of capital and labor in such forms as terracing
and water control projects). Most of the rest resulted from greatly
extending the cultivated area under double-cropping, i.e., from increasing yields per unit of cultivated land. The raising of two (or
three crops) of rice on paddy land, or winter wheat or barley followed
in the summer by millet or rice, was facilitated by the availability
of more workers (as a consequence of population growth) to meet the
peak labor demand when the first crop was harvested and the second
planted, and by water control projects (irrigation, drainage, and
flood control) which made possible a longer growing season. As a
by-product of the more rapid growth of population than land, the
availability of human and animal excrement--the chief fertilizers
employed in traditional Chinese agriculture--per mou of land also
increased.

The opening of new land, double-cropping, and water control
investments represented the application of increments of land, labor,

and capital within the traditional agricultural technology, rather than any new technological departures. Minor improvements in farm tools and methods of cultivation probably did occur over these four centuries, but the only important new technology introduced was improved (e.g., early-ripening) varieties of rice and two New World crops--corn in the sixteenth and potatoes in the sixteenth and seventeenth centuries. These technological changes accounted for perhaps ten percent of the increased aggregate output.

The Ch'ing economy before the nineteenth century--as I have stated earlier, agriculture represented the bulk of it--was thus not simply a "circular flow" system with little or no net investment. To be sure, the ratio of investment to national product was low when compared to "modern" economic systems. But before the possibilities of the traditional technology and the supply of land were exhausted, with a consequent onset of stagnation or decline, economic growth (but not "modern economic growth" which Simon Kuznets characterizes as the "spreading application of science to processes of production and social organization") was sufficient to support a population, a society, a state, and a higher culture that were at least the equals in size, complexity, sophistication, and quality of those of any European nation prior to the eighteenth century.

In the official Ch'ing land records, in addition to private land (min-t'ien), there were recorded the existence of substantial acreages, especially in north China and Manchuria, of banner land (ch'i-ti), military land (tun-t'ien), imperial manors (chuang) and the like which reflect the intention of the early Manchu rulers to superimpose a land system corresponding to the preconquest Manchu political and social structure upon that of conquered China. Even by the eighteenth century little in reality, apart from differential rates of land tax, remained of these earlier distinctions. The combined effects of population growth, inadequate official stipends to the banners, and the irresistable influence of the underlying Chinese system of private land ownership and the relatively unobstructed sale of land which had evolved in the T'ang and Sung dynasties had in practice almost entirely homogenized the various legal forms of land tenure. Banner land, as well as a substantial part of the min-t'ien, was farmed by Chinese tenants in small, scattered plots which by one or another subterfuge were freely rented, mortgaged, bought, or sold.

Neither land held under some form of official tenure nor private land was, other than in the exceptional case, farmed as a large contiguous estate with hired agricultural labor. Examples can be cited, of course, in any period of the dynasty of large landholdings by members of the nobility, officials, wealthy gentry, and monopoly merchants which exceeded say 10,000 mou; holdings of this size, however, were quite unusual. Ownership of land in Ch'ing China was skewed, but there were few large agricultural holdings comparable to the great estates of Europe and other parts of Asia, to the latifundia of South America, or the commercial farms of the United States. The landowner ranged from the owner-farmer cultivating perhaps 20-30 mou in north China and 12-15 mou in the south to a million or more elite families whose median holdings were perhaps 100-150 mou, much of which was rented to tenants. The figures just suggested are educated guesses extrapolated from modern data and from occasional references in eighteenth-century writings. We unfortunately have no useful information yet --perhaps it is impossible to assemble it--about the distribution of capital or income in China before the most recent period.

Quantitative data about the incidence and terms of tenancy in the eighteenth century must thus also be inferences from a later situation. The force of the more substantial qualitative evidence is, however, that the system of land tenure--patterns of ownership and tenancy--continued largely unchanged from the seventeenth century until at least well into the nineteenth. Individual families moved into and out of the categories of landlord, owner-farmer, part-owner, tenant, and landless laborer--but the relative sizes of these groupings were constant. Tenancy was much more widespread in the south (the "rice region") than in north China (the "wheat region"). Perhaps, as in later years, in China as a whole thirty percent of farm families could be classified as tenants and a further twenty percent as part-owners who worked rented land in addition to that which they owned. Rents were paid in money or in kind; if the latter, which was more common, they were usually fifty percent of the major crop in north China where share rents were more typical, but a fixed rent in kind rather than a share of the crop in the south. Fixed rents and generally longer leases in the south probably were conducive to more farm improvements by the tenants, and thus to greater productivity per unit of land. In the north where the share rent system and shorter leases provided a smaller incentive for tenant investments in farm capital, tenancy was also less common.

Given the fact that most small farmers were poor, living at a level of subsistence that left them always at the mercy of the inconstant weather, price variations, unexpected sickness, and the ritual costs of weddings and funerals, what checks were there on the further expansion of tenancy? The first step toward the alienation of a family's land was usually the necessity to borrow--at interest rates of 30 to 40 percent a year or more--funds to meet such crises and emergencies. Why then did the ownership of land not become even more concentrated in a few wealthy hands? The rarity of latifundia, the modal tiny family farm, and the widespread parcelization of farms into several nonadjacent fields usually of different qualities or types of land--these were in part the consequence of traditional inheritance practices, in particular the absence of primogeniture. For local elite and peasant alike, the death of the head of the family commonly was followed by the equal division of the patrimonial farm among all surviving sons who then established themselves as separate households. Fen-chia ("dividing the family"), as the practice was called, might be resisted for a generation or more, but the elite ideal of the large extended family did not often survive the inevitable tensions.

Investment in land, moreover, was limited by the relative absence in north China--where large cities were fewer and the typical overland transport more expensive than on the waterways of the south--of well-established markets for grain at which the landlord could convert his rent in kind into money or the tenant sell his crop in order to pay his rent in cash. Excessive concentration of landholding in the absence of modern transport and marketing, in effect, seriously depressed the income from investment in land. As it was, nineteenth-century data suggest that the typical return on land, after deductions for taxes and other costs, was only one-half as large as the 10 to 20 percent that could be realized from commerce and moneylending.

Within the limits set by fen-chia and the rate of return from renting land to tenants, "landlordism" and "tenancy" were significant features of the organization of agriculture. While not a barrier to the exploitation of the traditional technology up to its limits in the first part of the Ch'ing period, in the late-nineteenth and twentieth centuries--when increasingly the owners of rented out land were absentee landlords who did not reside in the rural areas--the land tenure system would be a major obstruction to the introduction of

modern agricultural technology. Rural class relations of course
were also far from idyllic even under the best eighteenth-century
Confucian landlord. The real burden of tenancy depended upon other
stipulations of the landlord-tenant contract in addition to the amount
and type of rent; and numerous examples can be cited of exactions
of labor services, "gifts," and onerous rent deposits. While the
political system and the ideology which justified it were still generally unchallenged, however, the social strains generated in the
countryside could be contained or repressed by the imperial state
with relative ease.

Handicraft Industry

The processing of agricultural products and the manufacture
of cloth, metal, wood, paper, and ceramic goods were carried on
either in handicraft workshops, predominately urban in location but
present also in rural areas, or in individual households both in urban and rural locations. The distinction between these two levels
of organization of handicraft industry is sometimes quite arbitrary
as peasant weavers, for example, in addition to employing the labor
of household members, might accumulate sufficient funds to purchase
one or more looms which were operated with hired labor. Or urban
craftsmen might similarly employ non-kin workers to supplement the
labor of family members in milling rice or ginning cotton. "Handicraft workshops" or "manufactories" (kung-ch'ang shou-kung-yeh)
were somewhat larger shops, essentially removed from the kinship
nexus and requiring the participation of the labor of probably un-
related members of several households. Examples of such undertakings include salt wells and refineries in Szechwan, copper mines
in Yunnan, pottery kilns like those at Ching-te-chen in Kiangsi, rice
and wheat milling in cities throughout China, and the calendering
and dyeing of cotton cloth in Kiangsu. No measure is or ever will
be possible of the absolute extent--the number of establishments and
their output--of this extra-household manufacturing. There can be
no doubt, however, that it was vastly overshadowed in both employment and output by the handicraft production of individual households,
either ancillary to farming in rural China or performed by full-time
urban and semi-urban craftsmen.

In the 1950s there was a considerable spate of publication in
the People's Republic of China which claimed the "handicraft workshops" to which I have referred as evidence of the beginnings--the

word used is <u>meng-ya</u> ("sprouts, shoots, <u>bourgeons</u>")--of "capitalist"
economic forms in China.   Indeed it was argued that embryonic
capitalism was flourishing at the end of the Ming dynasty and that
such men as Ku Yen-wu, Huang Tsung-hsi, and Wang Fu-chih (see
Section II) were its ideological spokesmen.   The Manchu invasion
set back this development a hundred years, but by the Yung-cheng
and Ch'ien-lung reigns incipient capitalist production was, it is
claimed, again flourishing within the dominant feudal society at a
higher level even than in the glorious days of the Wan-li reign in
Ming times.   Insofar as these writings remind us that the premodern
Chinese economy was not a stagnant and unchanging "natural economy'
--I have stated above that this was not the case in the agricultural
sector--they are of some interest.   But, with respect to their argument and the evidence which they cite, what the books and articles
on "capitalist sprouts" have done is to transplant wholesale to Chinese soil models drawn from a nineteenth-century understanding of
European history in an effort to demonstrate that Chinese society
too had developed, in conformity to the putative Marxist model, from
slavery to feudalism and then to capitalism.   Thus from a few possibly proven instances of fairly large-scale handicraft enterprises,
it is assumed that there were many more, and the hypothetical
many more are taken as proof of the flourishing of incipient capi-
talistic production.

Whatever "capitalism" may be, there is not the slightest reason for believing that these handicraft enterprises represented some
first stage on the road to modern industrial production, that China
too would have experienced an (entirely indigenous) industrial revolution if the West had not impinged upon it in the nineteenth century.
Most of the 132 references to workshops that have been culled from
eighteenth- and early nineteenth-century literary sources are brief
and imprecise and at best refer to enterprises that were very small
and served a limited local market; there is no support for the assertion that increasing numbers of peasants were forced from the land
into urban industrial employment by the concentration of land ownership; the internal organization of these enterprises so far as we can
tell showed no significant departures from the manufactories of the
T'ang and Sung periods; the technology of the workshops was entirely
traditional; and there is no evidence that profits were accumulated
for investment in improved capital.   There was more to the traditional Chinese economy than peasants, landlords, and rural villages,
but of course the same can be said of every other large "historical

bureaucratic society." In more recent years, P.R.C. historians themselves have abandoned this effort to make premodern China equivalent to premodern Europe; the implications of this position for the necessary role of the Communist Party in the modernization of China proved unacceptable.

The most important household handicraft in Ch'ing China was the spinning and weaving of cotton. Cotton cultivation was fairly widespread, but the principal producing areas were in the Yangtze valley provinces. It was in this region that cotton handicrafts were most concentrated and highly developed. Some areas in the Yangtze delta were better suited to growing cotton than food crops, and in the relatively humid climate of Kiangsu yarn of greater tensile strength and evenness could be spun. From Kiangnan (the area south of the lower reaches of the Yangtze river) and the districts around Shansi in Hupei, for example, quantities of baled raw cotton and woven piece goods were carried by water and on the backs of porters to North China, to Szechwan via the Yangtze, to Yunnan and Kweichow in the southwest, and to the southern coastal provinces. Spinning by rural households for their own consumption with supplies from the Yangtze valley and with local raw cotton was carried on to varying degrees throughout China. And locally woven cloth was supplemented by that which came from Hupei and Kiangnan.

In the chief cotton regions spinning and weaving in individual rural households was sometimes performed on a full-time basis, but more often it supplemented the growing of food crops upon which the family was chiefly dependent. The risks of total dependence on the market for one's food supplies were normally too great for very many households to specialize in handicraft production. Yarn, when not spun in the household, was obtained in exchange from the merchants who purchased the cloth which peasants wove above their own consumption needs. The income from textile handicrafts formed a larger part of the total income of poorer farmers with the smallest farms than it did of the more affluent. Preparation of the warp prior to weaving, for example, was commonly undertaken in small peasant households to supplement meagre agricultural incomes. The calendering and dyeing of cotton cloth tended to be concentrated in the market towns and cities which were also distributing centers for the finished product. These finishing processes were sometimes controlled by cloth merchants and performed by hired labor which was usually paid on a piece-work basis. Before the last quarter of the nineteenth century, the cloth merchants did not usually exercise any similar direct control over the weaving of the cloth which was commonly executed on their own account by peasant households. In the urban areas handicraft manufacture of cloth was under relatively strict guild supervision; the individual master craftsman with his apprentices and not the larger handicraft workshop was the dominant form of industrial organization.

Commerce

If we assume, I believe correctly, that the structure of the Chinese economy was not very different at the beginning of the twentieth century from what it was one or two centuries earlier, it is likely that in the eighteenth century 20 to 30 percent of the output of the agricultural sector (including rural handicrafts) was not consumed directly by the producers but marketed locally. At the most basic level, the peasants of every rural area bought and sold at the periodic markets (which were held at regular intervals, such as every third day) of the market town which served their group of villages. Here such agricultural surplus as they produced and the products of handicrafts manufacture were exchanged for other local commodities, or occasionally for goods of more distant origin which, in small quantities--only about five percent of farm output entered long-distance trade--had flowed down through successive layers of the nested marketing system to the final consumer. These thousands of basic markets--G. William Skinner estimates their number at 63,000 early in the twentieth century--were linked in turn to higher level intermediate and central markets, and to the major commercial cities.

In the modal case derived by Skinner for twentieth-century China--but which is suggestive too of earlier periods--the typical basic market ("standard marketing community") contained an area of about twenty square miles (52.5 square kilometers), with a population of 7,800 distributed in eighteen villages. The dependent villages were located in concentric circles around the market town and so distributed that the most disadvantaged villager was within easy walking distance (two to three miles) of the town. The standard markets, each of which in turn depended upon two or three higher level intermediate markets, were themselves typically perhaps six miles apart. At the periodic markets the peasants from the surrounding villages traded some of what they produced for other goods (e.g., oil for lighting, needles and thread, incense and candles for religious worship, pots and pans) and services (e.g., tool sharpening, carpentry, castration of livestock, barbering). Many of these goods and services were offered by itinerant merchants (peddlers) and craftsmen who made their headquarters in the intermediate market towns and travelled on a regular schedule among the periodic markets of the basic market towns. But the standard market would also have some permanent facilities of its own--a number of shops, and tea houses, wineshops, and eating places which were the centers of social intercourse on market days.

At each level the markets were populated by local merchants, and by agents of firms from higher and, except in the basic markets, lower level markets. At its higher levels--the central markets and above--the marketing system interpenetrated with the administrative hierarchy of the Ch'ing government. The larger and more complex markets were the loci of the important merchant guilds (ya-hang) through whom the bureaucracy regulated and taxed the commerce of of the empire. Here the local elite sold the grain which they had received as rental payments, and interacted in various ways with the local officials. In these superior markets, too, were found from the end of the eighteenth century the exchange banks (often operated by merchant families from Shansi province and therefore known as "Shansi banks") through whose drafts large government and private remittances were transferred from one higher level market to another. Other types of financial institutions, such as the "money shops" (ch'ien-chuang) which advanced funds to local merchants--usually on personal security and occasionally on the security of designated goods--as well as changing money from one local currency standard to another, were also located in the higher level markets. In the basic markets, barter was not unknown and the financial institutions were limited to the small money-changer.

The discreteness of the thousands of rural basic markets and the structure of the marketing hierarchy as a whole were closely related to the quality of the means of transportation. Higher level markets were located on or at the termini of the principal water routes by which goods and persons were mainly moved in south China or on main overland routes in the north, while basic markets were situated on the progressively less accessible feeder trails and waterways. Before the advent of the steamship and the railroad in the nineteenth century, long-distance trade was largely limited to high-value commodities (often for upper class consumption) and to the movement of tax grains from the Yangtze valley to Peking via the Grand Canal. The high costs per ton-mile of premodern transportation, the profits of multitudinous middlemen at each successive level of the marketing system, the frictions created by a bi-metallic silver-copper standard with multiple local currencies, and to some extent too the relative self-sufficiency in basic grains of much of rural China, were all limits on the development of a fully integrated national market.

Government and the Economy

The consequences of the Ch'ing political system for the Chinese economy have often been stated in terms of excessive and capricious taxation, omnipresent corruption, and a general disdain for commerce and the merchant. The fact is, however, that within the constraints of the traditional technology Ch'ing China was possessed of a complex and substantially commercialized economy which until the nineteenth century was able to support a growing population, the "pacification" of immense territories beyond the borders of China proper, and an unusually long era of internal peace, relative prosperity, and effective rule. While sometimes capriciously administered, in modern terms the tax burden on the population was light. Depravity found its place in China as in other societies, but no more so. If the merchant was devalued by the traditional ideological posture of "exalting agriculture and disparaging commerce," this does not negate the fact that he might be rich (the average annual profit of the Liang-Huai salt transport monopoly in the eighteenth century was perhaps 5,000,000 taels which was shared by thirty principal transport merchants and some hundred lesser dealers; an additional profit of 2,000,000 taels was divided among some thirty factory merchants); and powerful (in particular within the rural marketing structure where the local elite in and out of office invested in commerce and usury through his auspices); and fortunate (his sons and grandsons, with ample leisure and strict instruction--and perhaps an initial purchased title--might themselves enter the political elite). In sum, for the maintenance, extension, and prosperity of the traditional economy at a constant level of per capita output, the ideology and administration of the state were at least neutral factors and almost never, except in periods of dynastic decay, major obstacles.

To state this in another way, the traditional Chinese economy did not depend upon any direct economic role performed by the central government, or usually even by local officials, for its continuing operation and for such prosperity as it achieved. Discussion of the eighteenth-century economy in terms of modern macroanalysis of government fiscal and monetary policies, for example, even if the required data were attainable, would be anachronistic. China's premodern economy was not a single interdependent system, but a congeries of discrete local economies (exemplified by the marketing communities discussed above) which were contained in one political entity but only weakly integrated by economic ties. Government impinged on the economy by upholding the land tenure system, by some investment in water control projects, by taxing agriculture and commerce, through the government salt monopoly, and by maintaining internal peace and external security--but not in any other significant ways.

While Confucian theory might ennoble the peasant, or at least make the ruler sensitive to the dangers inherent in the existence of large numbers of discontented rural cultivators, he was even more acutely aware that the local elite landowners were the pivotal supports of the imperial state. There were accordingly repeated instances of imperial (rhetorical) efforts to aid the peasantry by encouraging land reclamation, providing some tax remission or direct relief in times of famine or flood, and even advising landowners voluntarily to reduce tenant rents when they had been favored by tax remissions. Imperial interference on behalf of the tenant, however, rarely went beyond this advice. In practice, the state strongly upheld the obligation of tenants to pay their rents in full and on time, even to the extent of placing it on the same legal level as the duty to pay taxes--which meant employing local police power to insure that rents were paid.

Most water control projects of the kind that I have noted were critical for the growth of agricultural output before 1800 were local undertakings for which in varying proportions the local officials shared the initiative and financing with the more wealthy and influential residents of the locality. There were few large-scale government projects, one of the major exceptions being the Yellow River Administration.

Its tax revenues were the major interest of the imperial state vis-à-vis the economy. Table 5 presents a recent estimate of the income of the Ch'ing government in the mid-eighteenth century. The land tax--i.e., a direct tax on agriculture--provided by far the largest part of the revenue (73.5 percent). It consisted of two components: the ti-ting (literally, "land tax and labor services combined") which was collected in silver, and the ts'ao-liang (grain tax, or grain tribute tax) which was still largely collected in kind in the eighteenth century. In 1712 the K'ang-hsi emperor fixed in perpetuity the official rates for the land tax; the provincial quotas due Peking were to be raised only as new land was opened and added to the tax rolls (increments which the provinces subsequently rarely recorded in full in their reports to the capital). Actual collections, however, continued to increase notwithstanding Kang-hsi's injunction. A number of devices were employed to enlarge the taxpayers' payments beyond the nominal quotas due Peking. One was the "meltage fee" (hao-hsien), in theory assessed to compensate for remittances of silver of less than the required purity and for losses in melting and casting silver ingots. As these losses were actually minimal, hao-hsien was effectively a tax surcharge in addition to K'ang-hsi's sanctioned rates. In 1724 this surtax received formal imperial approval and in part was thereafter remitted to Peking's account for payment to officials as an annual bonus to "nurture their honesty," i.e., to compensate for inadequate salaries. Other surcharges --for example, adding a sum for collection expenses to the taxpayer's bill, or manipulating the exchange rates between tax assessments stated in silver or grain and the number of copper cash per picul of grain or tael of silver which would be accepted as full payment of the tax due--although customarily accepted, were never formally sanctioned by the emperor. These revenues were not reported to the capital and were used largely for local administrative costs.

The estimates in Table 5 do not, I believe, include all of the additional "squeeze" from the taxpayer by yamen clerks and runners for the benefit of their own pockets, some of which, as I noted earlier, was "customary" and accepted by the populace while the rest was illegal and "corrupt." As these were not matters of record, it is impossible to state their amount with any degree of certainty. Studies of the lower Yangtze valley provinces in the early nineteenth century suggest, however, that the land tax collections reported to Peking were only a half or a third of the total actual

TABLE 5

CHINA'S ESTIMATED TAX REVENUE, 1753

(in 1,000 taels of silver and percentage shares)

Taxes	Amount Reported	Surcharges		Total	Share of Total (%)
		Authorized	Estimated Total Surcharges		
Land tax	43,775	5,151	10,439	54,214	73.5
ti-ting	30,419	3,549	7,098	37,517	
grain	13,356	1,602	3,341	16,697	
Salt Tax	7,014		1,754	8,768	11.9
Customs revenue	4,324	432	1,081	5,405	7.3
Miscellaneous taxes	1,053		4,352	5,405	7.3
Total	56,166		17,626	73,792	100.0

Source: Yeh-chien Wang, "The Fiscal Importance of the Land Tax During the Ch'ing Period," The Journal of Asian Studies, 30.4 (August 1971), pp. 832, 838, Tables I, III.

payments by the population to the magistrate and the yamen staff. Nor does the table reveal the essentially regressive nature of the land tax. In the haggling process which determined the actual payments made, the more influential local elite--the "great households" (ta-hu)--were in favorable positions to avoid some or all of the customary surcharges and most of the illegal squeeze by underlings. As a consequence the "small households" (hsiao-hu), that is, non-gentry taxpayers, paid at much higher effective rates per unit of land. In Kiangsu, for example, gentry households are known to have commuted their grain tribute obligations at a rate of 4,000 copper cash per tan ("picul," about 133.3 lbs.) of rice, while small households paid at rates as high as 10,000 cash per tan. Or in Hupei, the great households paid the grain tribute in kind in the official amount, while small households were required to pay in copper cash at commutation rates that doubled their tax burden. Poorer households, as a consequence, sometimes made arrangements with the more wealthy to have the latter pay taxes on their behalf at the more favorable rates which the wealthy could negotiate; the wealthy households took a middleman's profit in the transaction. This practice, known as pao-lan ("engrossment") was resisted by the local magistrates as it deprived the government of revenue, was generally favored by the yamen underlings who profited from arranging it, and benefitted the local elite financially and politically (as it made the small farmers dependent upon them). It serves as an excellent example of the real distribution of power in rural China. The probable real burden of the land tax on agriculture as a whole does not appear to have inhibited the steady growth in aggregate output described above. Its uneven incidence, however, was a continuing affront to the ideological emphasis on social stability.

Government control of the production and distribution of salt has a history going back to the Han dynasty (c. 119 B.C.). A consumption good required by all, but produced in quantity only in a limited number of locations, it lent itself easily to control and taxation. Before the mid-nineteenth century, the country was divided into ten salt zones for production and distribution. Most of China's salt was produced by evaporation from sea water or natural salt lakes; in Szechwan, underground salt brine was tapped by sinking wells to a depth of 1,000 feet or more; in a few other places salt was mined. The large investments required for producing and distributing salt were provided not by the government, but by licensed producers, factory merchants, and transport merchants who were closely supervised by salt officials. Factory merchants and transport merchants were granted monopoly rights respectively to buy specified amounts of salt from the producers, and to distribute salt (after acquiring it from the factory merchants) in defined areas. Annually the salt officials set quotas for production and distribution in each district which were expressed in terms of yin, that is, certificates permitting the holder to buy or transport a standard measure of salt. Salt merchants paid a substantial tax for each certificate, which constituted the government's revenue, and then proceeded to purchase, transport, and sell their salt to the ultimate consumers. In view of the inelastic per capita demand for salt, the salt tax-- which was passed on to the user by the sellers--was also a regressive one.

The salt monopolists, who were required to use their full allotments of certificates and thus provide the state with a specified tax income each year, were essentially tax farmers. In a sense the local magistrates who likewise had to remit stated quotas of taxes to Peking's account were also tax farmers. But unlike them, the salt merchants were private entrepreneurs dependent for their profits on the state of the market--including the ability of the government to curb the omnipresent smuggling of salt which made the salt gabelle fall far short of being an actual monopoly. Although the illegal trade might rival the legal, the monopolists' profits were (as the Liang-Huai region examples given earlier indicate) very large. Allotments of yin, in exchange for (illegally) sharing some of these profits with the salt officials, accordingly tended to become vested interests in the hands of a small number of wealthy families who might "sublet" their rights to the actual factory and transport merchants. The wealth of the salt monopolists and their dependence upon official recognition for their status made them frequent and unresisting "contributors" of substantial funds to the state to meet such emergencies as the suppression of the White Lotus Rebellion at the end of the eighteenth century. There were thirteen years between 1724 and 1804, for example, in which the Liang-Huai merchants were pressed to pay 1,000,000 taels or more to the imperial treasury.

The miscellaneous taxes in Table 5 included, for example, a levy on transfers of real estate, taxes on government-licensed brokers and on pawnshops, and local sales taxes on several commodities. Customs revenue came largely from coastal and riverine junk trade,

but was also levied at stations on several overland routes. In view
of the great increases in taxation on commerce in the latter half of
the nineteenth century, the burden of customs and miscellaneous
taxes in the eighteenth century must be considered quite light.

As we have no measure of China's gross national product in
the eighteenth century, I can only guess by extrapolating from much
later data that the share of total national income which passed through
the hands of the imperial government and its agents was very low
--perhaps seven percent, of which half was controlled by Peking and
half by the provinces and localities--but about what one would expect
in a premodern nonindustrial economy. The largest single expenditure to which these funds were directed, apart from the salaries
and maintenance of a relatively small number of officials and an
enormous multitude of clerks, runners, and the like, was on the
army of the empire. Regular annual costs of maintaining the banners and the Army of the Green Standard in the middle of the Ch'ien-
lung reign may have been about 17,000,000 taels. To this amount
must be added extraordinary expenditures for military expeditions
on China's borders and in Central Asia--I omit the White Lotus
Rebellion at the end of the Ch'ien-lung period--which have been
variously estimated at 120,000,000 to 150,000,000 taels over sixty
years, or an average of 2,000,000 to 2,500,000 per annum. Maintaining internal security and "protecting" the frontiers thus called
for a yearly outlay of about 20,000,000 taels, or more than a quarter of the total annual revenue estimated in Table 5.

The Structure of Society

Under this heading I shall describe some of the basic collec-
tivities as members of which most people--in other than their strictly
economic and political roles--spent the largest part of their lives.
In a peasant society like that of Ch'ing China, of course, the economic and political roles of the great majority of the population
were performed in or through the households to which they belonged;
structural differentiation in this respect was not very far advanced.
Further discussion of religious, ethnic, and linguistic minorities;
lineage organizations; and secret societies and heretical sects appears in my Rebellion in Nineteenth-Century China (Ann Arbor,
1975). Here I want to comment only on the spatial organization of
society, the institutions which participated in the "socialization" of

the population, and the composition and functions of the social elite, China's "gentry," to which I have already many times referred.

Spatial Organization

The first distinctions to make are between relatively full and relatively empty space, and between urban and rural settlement patterns. By the end of the eighteenth century, with the exception of Manchuria, virtually all of the territory which constituted the Ch'ing empire was fully used in terms of the population it could support at the then available level of technology. In addition to the the eighteen provinces of "China proper" whose area totalled roughly 1,370,000 square miles, the Ch'ing empire at its fullest extent claimed jurisdiction over other territories with an area of approximately 3,877,000 square miles. The late eighteenth-century total area of China thus was about 5,247,000 square miles. Even at the end of the nineteenth century, after considerable territory had been ceded to Russia, for example, Ch'ing China still embraced an area of approximately 4,278,000 square miles--some 600,000 square miles larger than the present area of the People's Republic of China, the difference being accounted for by Outer Mongolia which seceded from the Republic of China in 1912. Perhaps one-half of the Manchu empire was mountainous or semidesert with an average population density of less than one person per square mile. Less than one-tenth of the total area was cultivated. Ninety percent of the population lived in one-eighth of the country.

While these last figures are only approximations, they are sufficiently reliable to indicate how great a proportion of the eighteenth-century population was crowded into the north China plain, the Yangtze valley provinces, the Szechwan basin in the west, the southeastern coast, and along the West river (Hsi-kiang) in the south. These were the densely settled prime areas of China's modal intensive agriculture, while Manchuria was still largely virgin land, and the rest of the Ch'ing empire gradually shaded off into marginal agricultural land, and then into sparsely populated land in Mongolia and Central Asia suitable primarily for grazing. By the end of the Ch'ien-lung reign, if not earlier, China's landscape was a mature one with its population so distributed as to make maximum use-- by varying combinations of agriculture and animal husbandry--of the physical landforms, climates, soils, and water resources with which nature had endowed it. No major population movements--apart from the nineteenth-century settlement of Manchuria, and the significant increase of urbanization made possible by the introduction of the railroad in the late-nineteenth century--occurred after the first hundred years of Manchu rule during which, for example, the Szechwan basin was repopulated.

Again a rough approximation, at least ninety percent of the 300,000,000 people in China as of 1800 lived in rural areas, in villages or in small market towns, the rest in or very near towns and cities of, let us say, 10,000 population or greater. "Cities" (i.e., central places that were called ch'eng, literally "walled city") in Ch'ing China other than the capital (Peking) were, in descending order of importance, the sites of the yamens of the governors-general and governors, prefects, and chou and hsien magistrates. They numbered about 1,500 and varied greatly in size and importance, which was determined not only by their place in this political hierarchy but also by their position in a roughly parallel economic hierarchy which ranked urban conglomerations by the size of the hinterlands they served as marketing and commercial centers.

I have written "roughly parallel" because in fact there was no necessary correspondence between a city's political status and its size, wealth, and complexity. Many a hsien capital was hardly distinguishable in appearance from a large-sized market town of the kind described earlier in this chapter. Others were major commercial and cultural centers as well as being the seats of hsien and simultaneously of higher level (prefecture or circuit or province) government. Some significant commercial cities, on the other hand, were not included in the political hierarchy at all. The capital of a large and wealthy hsien or chou (which might also be a prefectural or provincial capital) would have a thick, high, and well-built city wall, or perhaps both an inner and outer ring of walls; a substantial military garrison; elaborately built and decorated public and private buildings; examination stalls where the imperial examinations were held; academies (shu-yuan) where famous local scholars lectured; and, if it were also a commercial center, markets, shops, numerous handicraft establishments, merchant and craft guilds, and financial institutions such as ch'ien-chuang. Prior to the late-nineteenth century there were few if any urban places that were primarily manufacturing centers--one might point to the important pottery industry at Ching-te-chen, Kiangsi, as an outstanding exception.

In the cities and in some of the more prosperous market towns could be found the "club houses" of the various voluntary associations based on common geographic origin (hui-kuan, "Landsmannschaften") which since the early seventeenth century had spread throughout China. Among other things, the hui-kuan provided a focus for recreation and religious worship (including burial of its deceased members), participated in the regulation of trade and the mediation of disputes, and normally made some provision for assistance to members in financial difficulty. By bringing together for common endeavors persons originally from the same localities but now resident in an alien city--either members of Landsmann guilds (e. g. , Ningpo merchant guilds in Soochow) alone or a broader social spectrum of men from the same home locality--these associations from one point of view enhanced the local particularism characteristic of Chinese society. But, perhaps more importantly and contrary to their localistic origins, the coexistence and necessary interaction of hui-kuan from many different places in a single city also contributed a degree of interregional social and economic integration to a society in which transportation was still slow and costly.

As I have already noted, large cities were found in greater number in the Yangtze valley and in south China than on the north China plain. The availability of water transportation in the south made it possible to supply food grains to urban conglomerations at transport costs that were only one-fifth to one-tenth as great as the cost of overland transport by mule and cart in the north. Moreover, both the danger of flooding by the Yellow river and the variability of rainfall in the north contributed to substantially less reliable annual crops than in the south, and introduced a precariousness to urban food supply which naturally limited the number of very large cities. Of the twenty-five to thirty cities with populations in excess of 100,000 in 1800, only five or six in addition to Peking--which was supplied at high cost by the grain tribute tax via the Grand Canal--were located in north China.

Only a few areas in rural China (in the regions of dense population) lacked agglomerated settlements--in parts of Szechwan, for example, where scattered farmsteads were the norm. The typical landscape was dotted with clusters of houses arranged along one or more streets which were surrounded by the village fields. So closely spaced were the villages in the areas of densest settlement that one

was often within sight of another. From the first part of the nineteenth century, in response to growing local disorder of which the
White Lotus Rebellion of 1796-1804 was only the most obvious sign,
many villages first in north China and then also in the south erected
protective walls around the houses and other structures in the village
center. In this sense the rural village was defined by the inhabitants
living within its earthen or brick walls, a situation closely related
to the circumstance that many villages were made up of populations
who possessed the same or a small number of different surnames
which corresponded to the lineage or lineages to which the population
belonged. The boundaries between the fields belonging to the inhabitants of one village and those owned by its closest neighbors were
not, however, so unambiguously distinguishable. In the course of
time farm land changed hands, and it was not unusual that the mort-
gagee (and possible eventual owner) of property in village A should
be a resident of adjacent village B, or even of village X at some
distance removed from A.

    Two comments might be made about the implications of this
indeterminacy of village boundaries which only began to change in
the last part of the nineteenth century when increased tax demands
by the hsien governments made it essential that the villages be
concerned about the precise areas in which the new levies would
be collected. First, while it performed other functions, it is doubtful that we should consider the rural village prior to the twentieth
century as always an operative political unit. A peasant's primary
loyalties were to his land (even if he had only tenancy rights), his
household, and especially in the south to his lineage. The formal
political leaders "or headmen" of the "natural" village--variously
styled hsiang-yüeh, ti-fang, ts'un-chang, chuang-t'ou, etc., and
appointed by the local official, but to be distinguished from the
pao-chia and li-chia heads which I discussed earlier who were also
official designees of commoner status--were commonly without much
real power. Most corporate decisions were made by informal leaders self-selected from the gentry heads of the prominent local lineage or lineages. In fact, I would suggest--not as a firm conclu-
sion but as a hypothesis--that the basic political unit in rural China
during the Ch'ing period was frequently the localized patrilineal
common descent group, i.e., the lineage (which is discussed further
below). This certainly seems to have been the case in south China,
and further investigation might show it equally so in the north.
The second observation is that while household and village were

natural social units and not artificially imposed by the state as the pao-chia and li-chia divisions were, the peasant's horizon was not bounded by them. The normal limits of person-to-person social interaction were not the village boundaries, but rather the borders of a higher order community composed of several (a dozen or a score) villages and the market town which served them.

Like cities, villages differed greatly in size and wealth and to a limited extent in function. In all of them by far the greatest part of the population were full-time farmers, though they or members of their households might also engage in off-season or ancillary handicraft activities. Some villages, while most of the population were still farmers, might include a number of full-time but small-scale handicraft and commercial specialists. Others--but not all--might contain the residences of local elite families, whose relative wealth (from tenant rents and various services) made possible leisure, a higher standard of consumption (including more elaborate housing), and the maintenance of such ritual edifices as ancestral halls. Regrettably we have no data on the distribution of villages in eighteenth-century China by population size. The following figures for early nineteenth-century Ting-chou, Chihli, are at least suggestive of the situation in north China: of 321 villages, 28 (9 percent) had populations of 1,000 or more, 198 (62 percent) had 200-999 inhabitants, 73 (23 percent) had 100-199 inhabitants, and 22 (7 percent) had populations of 100 or less.

A village community might be organized for self-defense (village walls and local militia), for water control (irrigation and drainage of the fields farmed by its inhabitants), religious activities (the villages in Ting-chou referred to above, with very few exceptions, all had one or more "temples"--some of these may have been ancestral halls), and education (a large and prosperous community might contain a school, although this was more likely to be a lineage undertaking than one of the village per se). And varieties of economic cooperation in the tilling of their fields among kin and sometimes non-kin villagers are well attested to. As in the case of the village school, most of these activities were under the effective leadership of the heads of the prominent local lineage or lineages, that is, usually of the local elite. Intervillage cooperation to these same ends--again under the supervision of gentry leaders, and mediated by actual or supposed lineage ties--was frequently undertaken. But parts of these and many other, more diffuse but no less significant, relations among the inhabitants of a group of interacting villages were also centered in the market town rather than in direct village to village contacts.

The basic market town which I described earlier in my discussion of commerce in rural China was not merely an economic center for the dozen or more villages which were dependent upon it. Together with its villages it constituted a "marketing community" in which the occasions of periodic marketing provided the opportunities for multifarious social relations among households beyond the confines of the village. In the tea houses and wineshops of the market town, the peasants of the several villages it served established the mutual knowledge and trust which made possible the rotating credit associations to which many belonged. Marriage brokers too operated in certain teahouses, and the marketing community as a whole rather than the village (which might itself contain only one exogamous localized lineage) presented the typical field in which mothers of marriageable sons sought potential daughters-in-law. The affinal relations established by intervillage marriages served to integrate the standard marketing community for other activities--local defense, crop-watching and irrigation, the planning and execution of major annual festivals, for example. As they interacted in the market towns, segmentary localized lineages of the same surname with real or assumed kinship ties, might be formed into larger composite lineages. Each market town usually also contained a major temple which was the ritual focus of the inhabitants of all its dependent villages. And the local secret society lodge would be located in the town too.

Not every village contained landed, leisured, and literate families, but some members of the local elite class were found in nearly every marketing community, which was thus a basic locus of the gentry's leadership and social control functions. In the tea houses, the social leaders of the community "held court" and mediated disputes among the peasants of the several villages. The basic markets towns, too, were frequently where the landlord collected his rents and dealt with his tenants. If, as was often the case, especially in the nineteenth century, the local elite had effective control over the remnants of the supravillage pao-chia and li-chia systems, the periodic markets offered the occasions at which they made their will known to the peasant population. And in the market towns, the (frequently) gentry officers of the secret society lodges met and made decisions which affected the entire community.

For the peasantry of premodern (and even twentieth-century) China, the basic marketing community was more than an intermediate social structure; it was itself a culture-bearing unit within the confines of which (rather than in their villages only) they carried on the central activities of the life cycle. Few peasants, however, normally went beyond its boundaries, which may be considered for our purposes the critical border line between local society and the wider world. Mediation between local society and the state--with the ambiguous consequences of simultaneously linking the one to the other but yet insulating rural China from direct control by the imperial state--was the function of the local elite to which I shall return presently.

Family and School

Biological dispersion of lines of descent in succeeding generations--a basic fact of demographic history--is incompatible of course with the maintenance of family status and property over long periods of time. Various kinship arrangements respond in different ways to the problem of preserving continuity. Primogeniture (which take one male heir to represent an entire generation) or preferential mating (such as cross-cousin marriage which leads theoretically to a situation in which all members of the society are kin), for example, will greatly enhance it. In most modern industrial societies, on the other hand, the prevailing kinship system sacrifices family continuity for other ends which the society values more. In premodern China, the patrilineal and patrilocal kinship structure may be said to have taken one step toward continuity, but in the absence of a further step (e.g., universal primogeniture) for any particular family the continuity achieved was an unstable one.

The empirical groupings in Ch'ing China which might be described by the English word "family" (itself a protean term) which is translated into Chinese as chia in fact displayed a considerable range of institutional arrangements. These, of course, were all constructed from the basic conjugal unit consisting of husband, wife, and children and designated fang in Chinese kinship terminology. In the often described developmental model of the family (chia), the "simple family" consisting of one fang and a single residence develops into a "stem family" as the adult daughters marry out of the family and one of the sons marries and has children. When a second son also marries and has children, a "joint family" of three generations in one residence is formed. Finally, at the death of the senior generation, the family unit consisting of two or more married brothers and their wives and children which survives constitutes a "fraternal joint family." It is perhaps unnecessary to stress that the above is an ideal-typical evolution, and not all families passed through this complete cycle, the last stage of which is fen-chia, division of the family and of the patrimonial estate, as a consequence of which the surviving sons, their wives, and children once again form simple families consisting of one fang each and separate residences.

Further complicating the ideal model and undermining the validity of some of the more simplistic surveys made in the twentieth century to determine the statistical frequency of these forms are the historical facts that members of the same chia did not always live in the same household; that after fen-chia, brothers and their several fang might continue to share the main rooms of the same residential building although they usually established separate cooking places; and that the members of the chia might not all derive continuous benefit from the estate or all be involved in the same set of economic activities. Both the historical and modern data are nevertheless sufficient to have long ago discredited the old notion that most Chinese lived in large joint families. This may well have been the ideal and desired form of family at least among the upper classes, but the conflicts of interest and notable tensions (among brothers in particular, and in various ways also connected to the relations among their wives) associated with living under one roof made it historically rare that a joint family would survive more than a generation. This reality is reflected in the demographic data which suggest five or six as the typical size of a Chinese family, although there was a likelihood that greater family complexity and size would be associated with greater wealth and social status.

On the other hand, the five or six were not exclusively organized as a nuclear family such as is typical of modern industrial societies. Nuclear familes (simply fang) existed--more often among tenant farmers and the poor than among the wealthy--as more rarely did joint families of some size and several generations--note the family of Chia Pao-yü in the novel Dream of the Red Chamber (Hung-lou meng). But the stem family and small joint family were also frequent phenomena. The association between family size and structure and relative wealth to which I have referred is related to the circumstances that poor families were less able to raise children to maturity, and that even when they survived to adulthood poor men, if they married at all, married later than the sons of the wealthy. Thus among the wealthy, marriage was likely to bring into the family several brides in each generation, but among the poor only one at best. And as the wealthy married at relatively young ages, the likelihood was greater than in poorer families that the eldest generation would survive until a joint family of three or four generations was formed.

Whatever its degree of size and complexity, the family was the basic economic unit for both production and distribution in rural China, functioned as a ceremonial group in what is frequently termed "ancestor worship," had the primary responsibility for the socialization of the young and for the care of the aged, and via the lineage provided a critical interface between local society and the wider world of the imperial state. Families agnatically descended from a common ancestor were included in more inclusive kinship groupings designated tsu for which the English term "lineage" (rather than "clan" or "sib") is the preferable translation. The degree to which lineages were formally organized (the extent to which they held common property, provided for the education and welfare of their members, maintained ancestral halls and grave-yards, compiled genealogies and rules of behavior), their size and complexity (the generational range and number of sublineage segments), and their localization (the tendency to be concentrated in one village or a small number of proximate villages) were unevenly distributed throughout China. There is some agreement that large, localized, and well-organized lineages were more characteristic of south and central China but also occurred in the north China plain. It is possible that this circumstance is historically related to the later settlement of the south, i.e., that it was more recently a frontier region in which survival and success were dependent upon effective group organization, and to the greater requirements for cooperative labor to develop and maintain the intensive irrigated rice-growing agriculture of south China.

Where lineage organization was strong and localized, it rather than the village per se may be taken as the primary political unit in rural China. While it was a cross-class organization which enrolled all persons regardless of status who had a common surname

and agnatic kinship ties, as a ceremonial unit for honoring its ancestors by worship of their tablets in the ancestral hall (to be distinguished from household worship which was restricted to the direct
line of the household head and generally extended back no more than
four generations), as a holder of common property (usually in land,
the income of which was used to maintain the ancestral hall, for
charity within the lineage, and possibly for educational expenses),
and as the locus for the mediation and settlement of intralineage
disputes, the lineage was dominated by those of its families who
had the highest social status and the greatest wealth. At least in
south and central China, it was thus a prominent vehicle for gentry
control of local society. Interlineage conflicts over water supply
or the control of the basic markets, for example, were among the
commonest "political" issues in rural society. A lineage's power
as against its rivals could be augmented if one or more of its sons
were successful in the government civil service examinations and
obtained a degree and possibly office in the imperial bureaucracy;
hence the "political" incentive to support lineage schools and promising scholars. And coalitions of nominally related lineages were
important means both for armed self-defense and for achieving and
perpetuating superiority over rivals.

Ancestor worship--both the domestic cult and that of the lineage
ancestral hall--while its specific rituals and eschatological assump-
tions were developed from eclectic popular religious practice rather
than from classical Confucianism, was promoted by and adopted as
a part of Confucian orthodoxy in imperial China. Neither the imperial government nor the Confucian literati were usually well-disposed
toward cultic religious practices which might develop into political
challenges to the dynasty and the social order (as Buddhism had
once been). Ancestor worship, however, was not merely accepted
but was legally prescribed even for Buddhist monks in the Ch'ing
law code. We have in this instance an extreme case of the general
functional utility of the diffused popular religious practices of China's
masses in sustaining the orthodox socio-political order. The traditional kinship system and the techniques of socialization associated
with it were strengthened by the ritual and emotion of the ancestor
cult, and in turn they reinforced the values of social harmony and
hierarchical order which were central to secular state and society
in Ch'ing China.

The role of women within both the family and the lineage was
distinctly an inferior one with respect to the formal distribution of

power and authority. Daughters married out of the families of their
birth (family of orientation) and into their husbands' families (family
procreation): the implication is that they did not share in the division of the patrimonial estate at the time of fen-chia. A woman,
that is, had no independent right to real property, although if she
came from a wealthy family of orientation she might have substantial
personal possessions. Within the family of procreation, the wife
was explicitly subordinated to the husband's mother and other
higher generation female relatives. In some cases young girls
(from poorer families) were brought into prospective families of
procreation years before actual marriage, and in the intervening
period occupied a status only somewhat higher than a household
servant. One exception to this general patrilocal practice occurred
in cases where the family of orientation had no surviving sons to
continue the family line, only one or more daughters. In this circumstance an eligible male (generally from a poorer family) could
be married into his father-in-law's family and adopt its surname.
While warm personal ties between husband and wife frequently
developed in spite of the fact that most marriages were arranged
by their parents with only the nominal consent of the partners, the
husband-wife relationship was theoretically and frequently in practice
of secondary importance to the collectivity-oriented relationship between parent and child--in particular between one male generation
and the next. Further diminishing the woman's status were the
incidence (probably exaggerated in the literature) of concubinage
among the upper classes, the prohibition against the remarriage of
widows, the limitation of the right of divorce to males, the practice (again primarily among upper class families) of female foot-
binding, and the occurrence of female infanticide among impoverished
families in times of great distress. These formal female disabilities
were partly, but not entirely, compensated for by the strong moral
encouragement in the traditional ethical system for filiality and respect for the aged. As the woman had sons of her own, became
a mother-in-law, and then a grandmother, her actual status and
power in the household correspondingly increased. But there were
no legitimate roles for the woman outside of her family before the
twentieth century. If this essay is almost exclusively concerned
with male actors, it thereby accurately reflects the society part of
whose modern history it seeks to recount and analyze.

In the traditional Chinese family a sharp discontinuity in the
treatment of the male child occurred between the ages of five and

seven. Until that time, when the child became old enough to perform simple farm chores or had matured enough to begin formal
schooling, he was treated with great indulgence and only light discipline. From that time onward the responsibility for his socialization was transferred from the indulgent females of his infancy to
his father and other adult males who made stern demands that he
acquire the social habits that would allow him to get along in a
world of material scarcity. Through a combination of physical
punishments and psychological sanctions, the older child learned
to depend upon hierarchical authority (but also developed an ambiv-
alence toward it), came to suppress outward expressions of aggres-
sion and hostility (but retained these emotions, which could be re-
leased against those subordinate in status and power to himself),
and accepted the demands of group solidarity (but simúltaneously
had internalized from the earlier indulgent years a sense of "self"
which sought gratification).

The authoritarian and hierarchical institutions of the traditional
Chinese political and social order were sustained by these patterns
of childhood socialization. Not only did they reinforce the explicit
social values of Confucianism which I discussed earlier, to which
only the literate social elite were directly exposed, but they under-
lay too the general political passivity of China's peasant majority
who could, however, in the face of extreme social strain erupt into
violent rebellion. The ambivalent political attitude of the Confucian
official toward the emperor, but his usual acceptance of even mini-
mally effective imperial authority; the passive deference of political
inferiors to their superiors, but their authoritarian treatment of
their subordinates; the sanction in Confucianism for the truly up-
right man to avoid all formal political roles--to pursue "self-
cultivation" rather than office; the fear of authority which kept local
officials from reporting accurately about disorder in their jurisdictions; the pervasiveness of the attitude of safety through conformity;
the elaborate mediation of social relations between political unequals
by rituals, gifts, and bribes; the general compliance with which the
authority of higher status was accepted within the lineage; and the
enormous hiatus between formal political authority and the daily lives
of most of China's population who were nonparticipants and only rarely
even amenable to "mobilization" to act collectively in their own in-
terests--all these manifestations of the traditional political culture
were products both of explicit political ideology and of the socialization practices which taught men how to be Chinese.

Primary socialization in the family was reinforced by the educational experience of the maturing male. If educated at all, females received instruction entirely within the household. For eighty or ninety percent of the population there was, of course, none of that formal education in which literacy was the basic skill and the classical Confucian texts the primary content (together with some history, geography, and postclassical prose writings). It should hardly be necessary any longer to discredit those idealized accounts of traditional Chinese education which wrote of a network of schools extending from the lowliest village to the capital itself in which even the son of a poor peasant might acquire the learning which opened the door to political office and social status. If China was governed by educated men, only rarely were they the sons of tenant farmers. The institutions that are usually referred to in this context--i.e., the prefectural, subprefectural, and district "schools" (fu-, chou-, and hsien-hsüeh) or the local "literati temples" (wen-miao)--were not in any case primarily places of study and learning. In Ming and Ch'ing times these were combinations of offices which registered and paid stipends to holders of the lowest degree (sheng-yuan), centers for educational propaganda, agencies which conducted the local examinations, and places for the worship of Confucius, the great teacher.

Elementary education was frequently provided in the household by private tutors, especially in well-to-do families. Organized local primary schools were of two types: the "community school" (she-hsüeh) which was supported by official and private contributions, and the "charity school" (i-hsüeh) which was founded and maintained by wealthy lineages for the sons of lineage members. What chiefly characterizes these institutions, although some were both long-lived and of excellent quality, is their uneven distribution (concentrated in wealthier communities), their ad hoc establishment and decline (there was no legal requirement to maintain them), and the smallness of their size, endowments, and facilities. The most important institutions of the traditional educational system--because they were more firmly institutionalized and better financed but again not legally required--were the "academies" (shu-yuan) which flourished both in the Ming and the Ch'ing. Large numbers of shu-yuan were established between the 1680s and the middle of the eighteenth century --one estimate suggests the existence of at least 4,500 by the early nineteenth century. The typical shu-yuan, however, was very small, enrolling 50 to 200 students. This flowering was the result of a

combination of official and private initiative and financial support.
The majority of the shu-yuan were probably not unlike the she-hsüeh
and i-hsüeh in that they concentrated upon preparation for the first
official degree. A smaller number of middle-level shu-yuan offered
(more thorough) preparation for the first degree, and also prepared
their students for the provincial examinations and the critical chü-
jen degree. A third and highest level, smallest in number and
usually located in provincial capitals, prepared primarily for the
provincial examinations, but also for the coveted metropolitan examinations. Headmasters and teachers in these academies were often
retired officials who rounded out their careers by instructing potential successors from their own local regions--a deed of merit in
Confucian eyes, but also a practical contribution to the welfare of
their locality which depended not a little upon the number and quality of the officials it produced.

Since their orientation was entirely to the government examination system, what the shu-yuan taught--in this the Ch'ing government strove for ideological conformity--was the orthodox Chu Hsi
interpretation of the classical texts. Not only content, but also
literary form and style were rigidly controlled, with a particular
emphasis upon the "eight-legged essay" (pa-ku wen) which in effect
played word games with quotations from the classics. The two
parts of the essay (each consisting of four "legs" or sections) were
respectively expected to present antithetical and balanced (in length,
rhythm, imagery, and diction) comments on one part of the quotation
in question. As there could be little divergence about substance,
the emphasis was heavily on form. It was altogether an authoritarian educational experience the intellectual results of which, if
not wholly trivial, were a reinforcement of the authoritarian values
of imperial Confucianism. Many complained about the idiocy of
pa-ku wen, but it persisted until almost the end of the dynasty.

The Social Elite

As we have seen, the Chinese village was not a self-sufficient
entity independent of the wider society. Economically it depended
upon some degree of exchange of commodities and services with
other areas. Politically it was too small a unit to protect itself
except against minor external threats; the effective use of force
required that it be regulated by the state over a wider area than
the village. And culturally, too, in its language, kinship and religious practices, style of food and clothing, and other social habits,

the village was part of a larger society--if not of China as a whole, at least of a substantial region in which a certain uniformity of mores prevailed. This integration, as I have also noted, was schematically a nested one in which smaller units--starting with the basic marketing community--fitted into successively larger ones. In China, as in other societies, certain social strata played specialized integrative roles, mediating between local society and the national (and regional) economy, polity, and culture in which they were also in various degrees participants. The rewards as well as the prerequisites of leadership were status, power, and wealth. Those who possessed it were the social elite for whom at various times I have also used the terms "elite," "local elite," "official elite," "bureaucratic elite," "literati," or "gentry." It is time now to comment on this terminology and on the societal roles of those to whom it referred.

The Ming and Ch'ing Chinese terms of which these several designations are translations are shen-chin or more commonly shen-shih. Shih and chin refer specifically to holders of government degrees while shen denotes an official. The most literal translation of shen-shih is thus "officials and degree holders," which also happens to be the most accurate single characterization of the social stratum which it defines. "Officials and degree holders," however, makes for awkward diction and the term "gentry"--in spite of its misleading evocation of an English country squire--has come to dominate the general usage, in part because members of the group referred to were frequently also rural landowners. "Literati," thanks to Max Weber, is also in general use and reflects the competence in classical literary studies which was a prerequisite for success in the civil service examinations and for eligibility to office. More recently the terms "elite" and "local elite" have been used to translate shen-shih or shen-chin. While in the interest of terminological rigor it may be advisable to dispense with the borrowed "gentry," "elite" is equally vague, and "local elite" although it accurately characterizes the great majority of the social group in question does omit its most prominent members. And I have heard, perhaps not in mere jest, the suggestion that we employ the neologism "intelligentry" as a solution to our terminological inconsistencies. The only way out of this morass is, I believe, by a combination of accuracy and convenience, which may satisfy no one but which I shall justify by referring to the actual composition of the shen-shih.

First, I must emphasize that I am characterizing the shen-shih stratum as it existed prior to the middle of the nineteenth century. A significant segmentation with portentous consequences for China's modern history occurred within this social group during the last decades of the dynasty. (These changes will be treated in another essay.) Next, the question to be answered is: in which of the several possible hierarchies of social stratification are we to locate the shen-shih? In any society the constituent population can be ranked by relative wealth, by the differential power which individuals command, and by a somewhat vaguer social status. Wealth in premodern China would refer primarily but not exclusively—there were as we have seen wealthy merchants—to agricultural property and income. Power meant overwhelmingly formal political power as a consequence of holding bureaucratic office. There were few private interest groups intermediary between state and society which were permitted to accumulate any countervailing power to that of the imperial state. Heterodox agglomerations of power—the secret societies, for instance—did exist, and sometimes seriously challenged the orthodox socio-political order, but by being dissident and heterodox they are excluded from the primary system of social stratification which is under consideration here. By social status I have in mind privileged leisure, participation in the higher literary and artistic culture, and a distinct (relatively luxurious) life style combined with general respect and deference from social inferiors and acknowledged leadership of community activities. To answer the question posed: I would suggest that while any particular shen-shih family or individual might rank high only in one or two of these parallel social hierarchies and that this ranking was a precarious one which might not survive more than a few generations, the group of shen-shih as a whole permanently occupied the top places (with the sole exception of the superior position of the emperor and imperial family) in all three.

Take the matter of wealth. Most shen-shih families owned land which was worked by tenant farmers, but some did not and the amount of land thus possessed varied from a little to a lot. For some shen-shih families their relative wealth was acquired as a result of their social status and political power, rather than being a precondition for them. Income ("squeeze") from local public works projects or the management of lineage estates, or the profits of high office, facilitated a step up in the hierarchy of affluence. Relatively poor shen-shih (e.g., some of those who were teachers in

local schools) were far from unknown, and many who were not shen-
shih also owned land--even in large amounts--or had substantial
commercial income. The categories of landlord and shen-shih thus
overlapped to a considerable degree but they remained distinct with
respect, for example, to the higher social status and potential access
to power which even a modestly well off shen-shih family enjoyed in
comparison to a wealthy family which merely owned land. The basic formal qualification for shen-shih status was the possession of
the lowest examination degree, or a title such as chien-sheng which
was nearly the equivalent, or official rank, or actual office. Normally rank and office were not available to those without an appropriate degree or title. Degrees (sheng-yuan, chü-jen, and chin-
shih) had to be earned by individual success in the government
examinations, but the chien-sheng title could often be purchased
as sometimes was also the case with (lower) ranks and (minor)
offices. Thus wealth, from commerce for example, might start
a merchant's son on the road to power but he first had to acquire
formal social status. And there remained an acknowledged social
distinction between those who had obtained shen-shih status via the
"regular" route, i.e., the examination system, and those who qualified by purchase, the "irregular" route.

When referring to the shen-shih as a whole (i.e., officials and
holders of degrees or titles), I use the terms "gentry," "elite," and
"social elite" interchangeably if only to vary my prose. On the
rare occasions when the word "literati" occurs, it should be taken
to refer to all those educated in the traditional manner including
degree holders and students who were aspirants for government
degrees. But the "gentry" or "elite" was also not an undifferentiated social stratum with respect to the amount of political power
its members exercised. The critical distinction to be made is between those gentry who actually held bureaucratic office, formerly
held office, or had earned the chü-jen and/or chin-shih degrees
which qualified one for appointment to an official post, and all the
rest--the much more numerous sheng-yuan and chien-sheng. For
the former (the shen), the terms "official gentry" or "bureaucratic
elite" are employed; the latter (the shih) I refer to as the "local
elite" or "nonofficial elite." This distinction also reflects the
spatial distribution in Chinese society of the members of these two
substrata of the social elite. The higher up in the nested and inter-
twined systems of administrative and marketing central places that
one goes, the greater the likelihood of encountering members of the

bureaucratic elite; while local society up to the level of the standard and intermediate marketing communities was precisely the home of the local elite. I have already given an estimate of the size of each of these gentry subcategories; together with their families, they constituted in all about two percent of China's population. This, together with the imperial household and the Manchu nobility, was the ruling class of Ch'ing China.

Earlier in the present essay the education and ideology of the gentry which were the media for their participation in a national culture were described. The ties of value and history linked even the most rustic shu-yuan to the intellectual and cultural life of Peking with intermediate stops in the district, prefectural, and provincial capitals. We have also seen the means whereby part of the elite came to staff the imperial bureaucracy in the capital and in the provinces and localities and how they functioned in office. And we have noted the leading role of the nonofficial elite in the economic, political, and social institutions of rural local society. In all their parts, state and society in Ch'ing China were permeated by the values and actions of this Confucian-educated, degree-holding, relatively wealthy, high status, official and nonofficial elite. If, as I have noted, the rise and fall of individual gentry families was part of the normal expectation in Ch'ing China, the gentry as a whole persisted and dominated all the key cultural, political, and (only to a lesser extent) economic linkages which gave Ch'ing society the unity and stability that it had even in the absence of modern means of communication. This perhaps is sufficient to justify our characterizing premodern imperial China--and in particular the Ch'ing empire, which far from being the nadir represented the highest development of what we think of as typically and tradition- ally "Chinese"--as a "gentry society." Political and social stabil- ity, which is the implied theme of this essay, and political and social change, which first came slowly and then with increasing rapidity and turbulence, depended above all else upon the fortunes of this small but omnipresent ruling class. While its values and its political and social roles remained unchallenged from within and without, traditional China continued along the course which the cen- turies had set. To change China required both that the gentry com- mitment to Confucian social values and the imperial political system which articulated them be somehow dissipated, and that the gentry monopoly of wealth, power, and status in local society be shattered. Lord Macartney's prognosis in January 1794, toward the end of his futile embassy to the court of the Ch'ien-lung emperor, was remarkably prophetic:

> The Empire of China is an old, crazy, first-rate man-of-war, which a fortunate succession of able and vigilant officers has contrived to keep afloat for these one hundred and fifty years past. . . . She may perhaps not sink outright; she may drift some time as a wreck, and will then be dashed to pieces on the shore; but she can never be rebuilt on the old bottom.[5]

But why not "rebuild on the old bottom"? Was it not possible to have a "modern" China--with universal political participation and representative political institutions, industrialization and a revolution in agricultural technology, rising living standards and popular welfare, participation (for good or for ill) in and increasing contributions to the homogenized culture and technology of the industrial world--while still retaining, at least in part, a gentry society?

From a very broad perspective--analytical and not teleological --it seems to me that the Chinese socio-political order which we have examined in this essay had made a critical and irreversible "trade-off" between a remarkably stable, effective, and universalistic political system which served a society that before the eighteenth century equalled or surpassed any other in its high culture, its social integration, and even in its satisfaction of the basic material and psychological needs of its population <u>and</u> the possibility of rapid adjustment to new circumstances in which that polity and society were no longer in perception or practical reality the "middle kingdom" of the "universe." The Chinese empire was never of course totally isolated from the non-Chinese world, but neither was it ever practically aware of any credible alternative to the way of the Sage Kings as this was expounded and implemented by their latter-day successors. In this circumstance, small changes and adjustments within the orthodox tradition both sufficed to respond to the problematics of the human condition and were all that was possible.

To do more, to attempt to reorder the polity and the economy in radical ways while still preserving the social dominance of the gentry, represented an absolute contradiction which could only result in failure or social collapse. For this ruling stratum was itself dependent upon the continuation of things as they were: to change meant to undermine that group which so to speak created and sustained the socio-political order itself. I have discussed, for example, the bureaucratically rational but superficial character of the imperial state whose writ stopped at the yamen of the district magistrate. Society below that level was led, governed, and sometimes exploited not by imperial officials but by the local elite. If large political and economic changes under traditional auspices were even to be attempted, the first requirement was that the central government be able to tap the economic and manpower resources of local agricultural society to an extent several-fold greater than the taxes and services it traditionally levied. In effect, the imperial government would have to penetrate and rule the rural villages directly rather than indirectly through the nonofficial elite. As the local gentry was as much dependent upon the state (for access to the examinations and to office, which were more secure means to perpetuate family wealth, power, and status than the mere possession of land and tenants in a precarious agricultural economy) as the state was upon it (for social control and the supply of recruits to the imperial bureaucracy), why did the imperial government remain only a superstructure over local society?

One answer, I believe, lies in the commonality of values and interests between those gentry members who directly served the state (the official elite) and their more numerous kin and friends of the same class who held no office. The ability of the Chinese state to recruit genuine "men of talent"--by its own standards, of course, which are not necessarily ours--was based upon the maintenance of the competitive civil service examinations as the main and most highly valued route to office. An individual's ability did count in initial performance in the examinations and in later progress up the bureaucratic ladder. But selection, advancement, and elimination according to ability involved a risk for a single family or individual even if the monopoly of office by the entire class of gentry was assured. The official career was the only route to power and status in traditional Chinese society, but even when high office was won it might, in the face of imperial whims, yet be an insecure status. Bureaucratic self-image and the interests of the ruler, as we have noted, did not always correspond. There was no development prior to the late-nineteenth century of highly valued economic or professional occupations which might be interchangeable in status with that of the imperial bureaucrat. Local gentry-dominated society in one aspect functioned as a "security blanket" for the aspirant to office who did not make it, for the retired or dismissed official, and for the Confucian idealist who resisted the emperor's raison d'état. The bureaucratic elite was no more prepared than the nonofficial elite to abandon the gentry's vested interests in dominating the local landed economy, its lineage leadership, its ability to "deal" with the local official and his underlings, its "public service" role, and its participation in local militarization. Those in office accepted in practice the apparent anomaly that the local gentry both supported the imperial state and prevented its penetration and reorganization of local society in the interests of the whole nation rather than merely of the gentry who actually ruled it.

NOTES

1. I shall usually refer to the Ch'ing emperors by their reign titles, either simply writing, e.g., "Ch'ien-lung" or more formally "the Ch'ien-lung emperor." See Table 1.

2. Quotations from Derk Bodde, "Harmony and Conflict in Chinese Philosophy," in Arthur F. Wright, ed., Studies in Chinese Thought (Chicago: University of Chicago Press, 1953), p. 68.

3. William Milne, trans., The Sacred Edict, containing Sixteen Maxims of the Emperor Kang-he, amplified by his son, the Emperor Yoong-Ching; together with a paraphrase on the whole, by a Mandarin (London: Printed for Black, Kingsbury, Parbury, and Allen, 1817), pp. 35-36, 39. The "Sacred Edict" is, of course, the 10,000 word Sheng-yü Kuang Hsün issued by the Yung-cheng emperor in 1724 as a commentary on the sixteen maxims or injunctions proclaimed by his father in 1670. These in turn were an elaboration of the six maxims of the first Ming emperor.

4. Quoted in Carson Chang, The Development of Neo-Confucian Thought (New York: Bookman Associates, 1962), vol. 2, p. 185.

5. An Embassy to China, Being the journal kept by Lord Macartney during his embassy to the Emperor Ch'ien-lung, 1793-1794, edited with an introduction and notes by J. L. Cranmer-Byng (London: Longmans, 1962), pp. 212-213.

SUGGESTIONS FOR FURTHER READING

Bodde, Derk and Clarence Morris. Law in Imperial China. Cambridge: Harvard University Press, 1967.

Chang, Chung-li. The Chinese Gentry. Seattle: University of Washington Press, 1955.

Ch'ü, T'ung-tsu. Local Government in China Under the Ch'ing. Cambridge: Harvard University Press, 1962.

de Bary, Wm. Theodore, ed. The Unfolding of Neo-Confucianism. New York: Columbia University Press, 1975.

Fairbank, John K. and S. Y. Teng. Ch'ing Administration: Three Studies. Cambridge: Harvard University Press, 1960.

Ho, Ping-ti. The Ladder of Success in Imperial China: Aspects of Social Mobility, 1368-1911. New York: Columbia University Press, 1962.

_____. Studies on the Population of China, 1369-1953. Cambridge: Harvard University Press, 1959.

Hsiao, Kung-ch'uan. Rural China: Imperial Control in the Nineteenth Century. Seattle: University of Washington Press, 1960.

Kahn, Harold L. Monarchy in the Emperor's Eyes: Image and Reality in the Ch'ien-lung Reign. Cambridge: Harvard University Press, 1971.

Lee, Robert H. G. The Manchurian Frontier in Ch'ing History. Cambridge: Harvard University Press, 1970.

Liang, Ch'i-ch'ao. Intellectual Trends in the Ch'ing Period. Translated by Immanual C. Y. Hsü. Cambridge: Harvard University Press, 1959.

Metzger, Thomas A. The Internal Organization of the Ch'ing Bureaucracy: Legal, Normative, and Communications Aspects. Cambridge: Harvard University Press, 1973.

Michael, Franz. The Origin of Manchu Rule in China. Baltimore: Johns Hopkins University Press, 1942.

Nivison, David S. The Life and Thought of Chang Hsueh-ch'eng (1738-1801). Stanford: Stanford University Press, 1966.

Oxnam, Robert B. Ruling from Horseback: Manchu Politics in the Oboi Regency, 1661-1669. Chicago: University of Chicago Press, 1974.

Pei, Huang. Autocracy at Work: A Study of the Yung-cheng Period, 1723-1735. Bloomington: Indiana University Press, 1974.

Perkins, Dwight H. Agricultural Development in China, 1368-1968. Chicago: Aldine, 1969.

Rozman, Gilbert. Urban Networks in Ch'ing China and Tokugawa Japan. Princeton: Princeton University Press, 1973.

Spence, Jonathan D. Emperor of China: Self-Portrait of K'ang-hsi. New York: Knopf, 1974.

_____. Ts'ao Yin and the K'ang-hsi Emperor: Bondservant and Master. New Haven: Yale University Press, 1966.

Wang, Yeh-chien. Land Taxation in Imperial China, 1750-1911. Cambridge: Harvard University Press, 1974.

Watt, John R. The District Magistrate in Late Imperial China. New York: Columbia University Press, 1972.

Wu, Silas H. L. Communication and Imperial Control in China: Evolution of the Palace Memorial System, 1693-1735. Cambridge: Harvard University Press, 1970.

MICHIGAN PAPERS IN CHINESE STUDIES

No. 1. The Chinese Economy, 1912-1949, by Albert Feuerwerker.

No. 2. The Cultural Revolution: 1967 in Review, four essays by Michel Oksenberg, Carl Riskin, Robert Scalapino, and Ezra Vogel.

No. 3. Two Studies in Chinese Literature, by Li Chi and Dale Johnson.

No. 4. Early Communist China: Two Studies, by Ronald Suleski and Daniel Bays.

No. 5. The Chinese Economy, ca. 1870-1911, by Albert Feuerwerker.

No. 6. Chinese Paintings in Chinese Publications, 1956-1968: An Annotated Bibliography and an Index to the Paintings, by E. J. Laing.

No. 7. The Treaty Ports and China's Modernization: What Went Wrong? by Rhoads Murphey.

No. 8. Two Twelfth Century Texts on Chinese Painting, by Robert J. Maeda.

No. 9. The Economy of Communist China, 1949-1969, by Chu-yuan Cheng.

No. 10. Educated Youth and the Cultural Revolution in China, by Martin Singer.

No. 11. Premodern China: A Bibliographical Introduction, by Chun-shu Chang.

No. 12. Two Studies on Ming History, by Charles O. Hucker.

No. 13. Nineteenth Century China: Five Imperialist Perspectives, selected by Dilip Basu, edited by Rhoads Murphey.

No. 14. Modern China, 1840-1972: An Introduction to Sources and Research Aids, by Andrew J. Nathan.

No. 15. Women in China: Studies in Social Change and Feminism, edited by Marilyn B. Young.

No. 16. An Annotated Bibliography of Chinese Painting Catalogues and Related Texts, by Hin-cheung Lovell.

No. 17. China's Allocation of Fixed Capital Investment, 1952-1957, by Chu-yuan Cheng.

No. 18. Health, Conflict, and the Chinese Political System, by David M. Lampton.

No. 19. Chinese and Japanese Music-Dramas, edited by J. I. Crump and William P. Malm.

No. 20. Hsin-lun (New Treatise) and Other Writings by Huan T'an (43 B.C.-28 A.D.), translated by Timoteus Pokora.

No. 21. Rebellion in Nineteenth-Century China, by Albert Feuerwerker.

No. 22. Between Two Plenums: China's Intraleadership Conflict, 1959-1962, by Ellis Joffe.

No. 23. "Proletarian Hegemony" in the Chinese Revolution and the Canton Commune of 1927, by S. Bernard Thomas.

No. 24. Chinese Communist Materials at the Bureau of Investigation Archives, Taiwan, by Peter Donovan, Carl E. Dorris, and Lawrence R. Sullivan.

No. 25. Shanghai Old-Style Banks (Ch'ien-chuang), 1800-1935, by Andrea Lee McElderry.

No. 26. The Sian Incident: A Pivotal Point in Modern Chinese History, by Tien-wei Wu.

No. 27. State and Society in Eighteenth-Century China: The Ch'ing Empire in its Glory, by Albert Feuerwerker.

Prepaid Orders Only

MICHIGAN ABSTRACTS OF CHINESE AND
JAPANESE WORKS ON CHINESE HISTORY

No. 1. The Ming Tribute Grain System, by Hoshi Ayao, translated by Mark Elvin.

No. 2. Commerce and Society in Sung China, by Shiba Yoshinobu, translated by Mark Elvin.

No. 3. Transport in Transition: The Evolution of Traditional Shipping in China, translations by Andrew Watson.

No. 4. Japanese Perspectives on China's Early Modernization: A Bibliographical Survey, by K. H. Kim.

No. 5. The Silk Industry in Ch'ing China, by Shih Min-hsiung, translated by E-tu Zen Sun.

NONSERIES PUBLICATION

Index to the "Chan-kuo Ts'e", by Sharon Fidler and J. I. Crump. A companion volume to the Chan-kuo Ts'e, translated by J. I. Crump (Oxford: Clarendon Press, 1970).

Michigan Papers and Abstracts available from:
Center for Chinese Studies
The University of Michigan
Lane Hall (Publications)
Ann Arbor, MI 48109   USA

Prepaid Orders Only
write for complete price listing